LIVE
LIFE
FULLY

Pat Renner
1 John 5:13

LIVE LIFE FULLY

Make Every Day Count by Centering on God

PAT RENNER

TATE PUBLISHING
AND ENTERPRISES, LLC

Published by Tate Publishing & Enterprises, LLC
127 E. Trade Center Terrace | Mustang, Oklahoma 73064 USA
1.888.361.9473 | www.tatepublishing.com

Tate Publishing is committed to excellence in the publishing industry. The company reflects the philosophy established by the founders, based on Psalm 68:11,
"The Lord gave the word and great was the company of those who published it."

Book design copyright © 2011 by Tate Publishing, LLC. All rights reserved.
Cover design by April Marciszewski
Interior design by Sarah Kirchen

Published in the United States of America

ISBN: 978-1-61346-699-5
1. Religion / Christian Life / Inspirational
2. Religion / Christian Life / Women's Issues
11.09.28

TABLE OF CONTENTS

INTRODUCTION

I want to write this book for my family and for all those who think they have a lot of time left. I want to tell everyone how short life really is. This book will give you a new look at life by looking back at life and not forward. Oh, I'm not dying, but I am growing older each day. Things are starting to fail, and I am slower than I used to be. I can hardly believe I am over sixty and have two married sons in their forties and three wonderful grandchildren. I have been around long enough to have lived in my home over thirty-six years and be married for over forty-five years. It only seemed like yesterday that I walked down the aisle to be married or entered the hospital to give birth to my first son. Now, it is only a few years later, and my life has passed by so quickly. I made history in my walk on this earth.

While you are living in your busy life, it may seem like there is a lot of time to do the things you want to do. I cleaned my basement a few months ago and found a baby blanket I thought I would finish after my first son got a little bigger. Well, time is short, and there is certainly not enough of it to go around. I put the unfinished blanket in a garage sale; there never will be enough time to finish it now, forty years later.

It seems like a couple of years ago my own babies were playing in the living room with their trucks. It is amazing, all the friends I had and fun things I did were so long ago. When I looked forward then, old age seemed so far away, but when I look backward now, life is so short.

I regret nothing, because I wrote this book to encourage everyone who reads it to live your life, and dream your dreams, and put God in the middle of it all. I don't want anyone to say when it is all over, "I wish I would have done this or that." We need to serve the Lord with our life and when our lives are through did we live our lives for you (God)?

I pray this book can teach you to live and love and serve one another, so that you do not waste your days with anger, fear, depression, or boredom. I want you to know life with God's presence in it. I had few tears in my life that were sad or unhappy, but the tears I cried were ons of joy and happiness because Jesus was in my life.

I have a lot of life to live yet, but my life story is full of pages that must be written about Jesus, and time is short. May this book bless you as you learn to live life fully for the Lord.

—Patty

REVELATION 3:16

"But because you are lukewarm, neither hot nor
cold, I am going to spit you out of my mouth!"

Every word in the bible is true. So are these words from Revelations. God will cast away people who are lukewarm about Him. He will spit them out. We all must take a stand. Decide which one you are. Hot for Him or cold against Him. Think about being cast out of His presence, life without God. Don't spend your life in the lukewarm mode not really caring about anything. Become bold and stand strong for God. Don't be afraid because God will always be there for you if you are Hot for Him. Get involved with His word. Have conversations with Him in prayer. Tell all your friends about God and His precious Son Jesus. Cover yourself with God's presence. Let every moment of your life be one that brings glory to God. Then you will become that Hot Christian God is speaking of in this verse. Learn to live your life fully for God.

WRITING 101

I love to write, it makes me feel complete just to express myself on paper. In January 1994, I picked up a pen and wrote my first writings. I don't know what to call all of them, are they stories, devotions or homilies, but I have over one hundred of them now. I am not a writer. I wasn't good in English Comp when I was in high school many years ago. So what happened? I have not finished college and I always had trouble just writing a letter to someone. My brother Dave, the writer, sent my letters back to me with corrections. Now, I want to write my thoughts down on paper.

One January I was looking at the pussy willow tree in my backyard. I could almost touch the branches from my window. I was thinking about this tree when I was compelled to write my thoughts down. Now every time I have deep thoughts, I write them down on paper.

I didn't realize this was the way God would protect me in the coming months. The next thing I wrote was a love letter to Jesus. I had times in my life that I needed God to handle. I wrote about God and his love and strength in my life. When my father was ill I wrote about trusting God. The stories all started with a thought and ended with Jesus. They were about seeking the face of Jesus or about how He would never leave us alone. I wrote about how all my strength came from the Lord. When I wrote, a peace came over me because I was in the presence of the Lord.

I began to write about my inner most feelings. Some stories were written during very bad times in my life. Between the stressful stories of pain and agony, I wrote peaceful stories that were calm and secure stories of God's love. I wrote about times I trusted God.

When I read the stories, I can't believe I wrote them, they are so rich with God's presence. I am compelled to write although there was years I could not write a word. I was a C average English student who now writes thousands of words only by the grace of God.

God's Creation

As I was sitting by my window one cold, frosty January morning, I saw the silhouettes of trees, bare, and lifeless. Tears welled up in my eyes because the trees look empty and alone, this made me reflect upon my own life. I once was empty, bare, lifeless, and alone. When I looked closer at that lifeless tree, the branches had buds on them that were swelling with life; leaves would soon bring life to this tree.

I needed something to burst out of me and bring me new life too. This was a time to trust in God and His word, to let Him be the Lord of my life. I was taking the lead in my life, and it looked dead, and lifeless, my decisions lead me to a place that was barren and alone. I needed to let God fill me with His marvelous grace and love.

As the buds would get larger and larger on this tree and then burst open to become new leaves, so it was with my life. As my love for God grew larger and larger, and I began to trust Him more and more, I longed to be near Him and to know His word. I grew stronger in my faith. I was being filled, and new life was ready to burst forth.

My heart raced with joy. It was spring and it was a time to reflect on Christ and His love for me. Easter was nearing and this was the time God gave up His Son for me. God's gift to me was Jesus. He died on that Friday so that on Easter morning, He could rise again and conquering death, and then I would live forever. This was the greatest gift anyone could give me. Oh, what a love God has for me. I am special to God, and loved by Him. God has made me strong in my weakness. His word promises that,

> My grace is sufficient for you, for my power is perfected in weakness.
>
> 2 Corinthians 12:9

God changed me from bare, lifeless and alone, to powerful, perfect and strong by His grace.

Soon the flowers would be peeking out of the ground reaching to the heavens and I thank God for this time to reflect. It says in the Song of Solomon,

> See! The winter is past; the rain is over and gone. Flowers appear on the earth; the season of singing has come.
>
> Song of Solomon 2:11–12

God gives His trees leaves, fullness, and strength, and they all reach up to Him in return. The leaves on the trees don't falter or fall, they are held strong through the winds and storms of life. With God's love in me, I am like the tree; I am covered and protected by God. God is always strong in my life if I follow Him and trust Him and reach up to Him for the rest of my life.

The sunlight helps the trees to grow straight and tall, they get stronger with the suns light. As I grow in Christ, I too get stronger each day with the Son's light shining within me. Jesus is the light of my life to warm my heart and give me peace and joy. As it is with the trees in the fall, the leaves will turn brilliant colors, painting the hillsides. The leaves mature and reach the fullness God has planned for them. They are all shades of gold, and God has completed His work in them. I pray God's work will be complete in me one day, and I will be a brilliant shade of gold when I die.

Robins

The songs of the birds are so peaceful. The air has an aroma of flowers. Praises to God, the maker of my earth, I have peace here. The birds even bring a sense of peace as they hop on the ground looking for that special worm. They are fed by God's hand, and they trust Him.

Today I will trust in the Lord and remember that God will provide all my needs. I will see God in the beauty of the trees, grass, flowers, and birds. I will find peace in the Lord; He will be my resting place. With this peace, I will pray thanking God for all that has been given me because God's Son Jesus won the victory for me. Oh ,how I love God for all He has done for me.

The birds are still singing and the peace of God is all around I have stillness in my heart. I am safe and at peace.

March Snows

As I write, this day is gray, so gray. Overcast, they say, with twelve inches of snow on the ground. Most of this day, there was silence surrounding me. How do I know God is here? The mounds of bellowing snowdrifts acknowledge God's presence. The day is beautiful, and the cardinals and blue jays jump from tree to tree playing with each other.

God is almighty, and His presence is in every snowflake, each one special, and each one different. God's people are special to Him, and He created us all different and individual just like the snowflakes.

Today the sky has no sun, only grayness and snowflakes. Where is the hope we look for each day? It does not come from the sunlight; it comes from God's Son's light shining in our lives. God's Son brings us hope for each new day. When I look at the clouds, I know there is sunshine above them, if I climb high enough, and I know the sun is shining every day of my life. The clouds above the darkness are white and fluffy. The sun above the gray clouds is so bright one can hardly see.

I always want to keep the vision of sunshine above the dark clouds. I want to know that God's Son brings hope to me each day, and I never judge the day by how gray it is. I thank God for gray days and rainy days. I thank Him for the clouds and the sunshine too. I thank Him for the March snow knowing the spring flowers are underneath.

The Garden

I am the true vine; my Father is the gardener.

John 15:1

We all have gardens. We plant and we fertilize and we water. We hoe the weeds out when they start to take over the area. Sometimes our plants look like they will die so we give them extra care and attention. The sun shines on our gardens to help the plants grow strong and mature to produce a good crop. Then we harvest our crop; this is the whole purpose of our garden.

That is the way it is with us. The Bible says we are the branches and Jesus is the vine. But, God is the gardener; He trims and cleans every branch. He cuts out the bad branches; the Bible says He prunes us. He doesn't want sin to take over our lives, so He gives us special care and attention. As we walk with Him, He gives us His word and His Spirit to help us grow strong in the Lord.

God wants us to produce good fruit. We cannot produce fruit away from the Vine, Jesus. God tends to us and cares for us because He wants us to mature in our faith. He wants us to be like the Vine.

The Gardener wants us to tell others about Jesus. This is the fruit we will bear. He wants all people to know His grace. When others come to know the Vine, they too can produce good fruit. After all, that is the purpose of God's garden, to produce a mature crop. Then God will reap the harvest. His crop will be the new believers in Jesus Christ. He will gather His crop and take them home to heaven one day. Just let the Son shine on you and you will grow in your faith. Let the Gardener care for you as you grow. Then you too will produce good fruit.

Friends Forever

I have a good friend. She was just a friend until recently when she became a good friend. What's the difference you may ask? Well, let me try to explain. She always has a smile and a twinkle in her eye, so she is easy to like. We were brought together by mutual friends, and later we became closer when we were in a Bible study. I considered her my good friend.

Oh! I have a lot of friends, maybe more than most, but very few good friends. Let me tell you what a good friend is. She builds you up and does not consider herself first. She shows you her love by doing acts of kindness, and puts your wishes before hers. She loves you with the love that can only come by knowing a Savior. She follows Ephesians 4,

> Be kind and compassionate to one another, forgiving each other, just as in Christ God forgave you.
>
> Ephesians 4:32

I love people because God loves me. I would do anything for them to know Christ a little more. All I have to give to others is my love. Friends need to lift one another up with the help of God. The indwelling Spirit of God helps to remind me of someone in need. I thank God for the gentle reminders of how to be a good friend.

My good friend is an encourager, and sometimes I need that. I also need the prayers she prays for me in times of trouble. She offers help to me that will lighten my load. When she went to the store for me, she picked up my necessities and surprised me with a banana as a treat. When I ate the banana, I thanked God for my good friend. When God's people do kind things for one another and serve one another, they are serving God. God knows what we need and God provides good friends.

We Shall Be Changed

Dear friends, now we are children of God and what we will be has not yet been made known. But we will know that when he appears, we shall be like Him for we shall see Him as He is. Everyone who has this hope in him purifies himself just as He is pure.

1 John 3:2–3

What is the future for a Christian? 1 John 3:2–3 tells us great changes are going to happen when Christ comes, but the greatest change is going to be the change in us! We shall be like Him!

Look at a caterpillar on a dusty road. It is not yet clear that it shall become a beautiful butterfly flitting from flower to flower in your garden. Look at the rose root you purchased from the grocery store, it is not yet clear that from this dry root there will come a beautiful, fragrant rose. Look at your life as a new child of God on this earth. It is not yet clear what you will become. This verse tells us we shall become like Him! Every day we become more like Jesus and one day in Glory, we will be just like Jesus. The very thought of this miracle stimulates us to behavior which is more pure and Holy.

What does it mean to be like Him? How will we be different? The change begins the moment we are saved by Jesus' death.

It is a slow process, which will take the rest of our natural lives on earth. God is at work in us. God wants us to be more like Jesus every day. That is why he came in human form to show us the way we should act.

We must love one another with a love that is unconditional. We should love the unlovely people. We should help the helpless with whatever they need. Our kindness should be in abundance. We should want everyone to know the love God has for them. We should have the fruits of the spirit in our lives.

When God sent His one and only Son to die for us on that cross, Jesus traded lives with us. He took on our sin and we were left with His Spirit living in us so we could be like Him, a new creation, the Bible says. That is how we can live and love like Jesus because we were changed on the inside the moment we come to know Him. We are made righteous by the blood of the Lamb, Jesus.

When we are changed, we do things differently. What we thought was fun, but was sin, we no longer love. We long to worship God at His house and praise His holy name. We would rather read His word than any other words. We are obedient to God's commands. We are changed like the caterpillar and made beautiful in God's sight like the rose. We were the dead-looking rose roots, but God made us come to life in Christ and bloom in our spiritual life. We are new creations.

The Bible promises that when He appears, we will be changed on the outside and we will look different. We will have a glorified body and we will know Him as He is. We will be made perfect, as He is perfect. This is the plan God has for you and for me to live forever. When this happens, we will be with Him forever in paradise. All I can say is, "Hallelujah! Come Lord Jesus."

The King Is Coming

While we wait for the blessed hope, the glorious appearing of our great God and Savior, Jesus Christ.

Titus 2:13

Every morning when I wake up, I praise God for another day as I get up and make my way to the door to look out on the beautiful day. The sky always speaks God's presence to me. Whether it is cloudy or blue, it is God's day!

Most people would be looking to see what kind of weather this day would bring. Their concern is how they should dress. What will the temperature be? Will it be cold or rainy? Will the sun shine or will the day be gray? Will this day make them happy or gloomy? But when I look up towards the heavens, I look for the blessed hope and the glorious appearance of my Lord and Savior Jesus Christ. The promise is in Titus chapter two, and it is for me and for you.

The time the earth has left is a short time compared to eternity. But the promise is, Jesus will return for all believers. We don't know the time when He will come back, but we know He will. He will come in the clouds to meet His saints in the sky. This is His promise to us. Waiting for the glorious appearing, it is my desire to be among the people who meet Him in the clouds.

He is coming for sure so we must let everyone know what the Bible says. We must not let them perish without a Savior. Life is not just about living day to day for you and for me. There are people who will not be with us in the clouds, the bible tells us in 1 Thessalonians 4:17. People who were our friends will not be there. People, who do not know His promises, will not be there. We need to tell them all, we need to feel the urgency of Christ's return.

He Is Coming!

I long to be in His presence. I long to see Him face to face. The longer I stay on the earth, the more fervent my love is for the Lord. Every day I look to the sky expecting to see the risen Lord returning for me. Is it today, or will it be tomorrow when He returns? Will I meet the King of Kings and Lord of Lords before the week is out? My heart's desire is to be with Him forever.

One day I will see Him face to face, and you can too. All we need to know is Jesus Christ came to earth to die on the cross to save all people for their sins. We need to believe Jesus died for us. We need to know He ascended into heaven and sits on the right hand of God almighty. Do you believe this?

My prayer for you is, as the Bible says, for Jesus to dwell in you richly. If you know Jesus as your Lord and Savior, your heart will change. Then, when you look into the sky, you too will see the Master's return. Keep looking for the blessed hope of the world. He wants to live forever with you and with me. He longs for us to be His children. The children of His promise will look into the sky tomorrow and wait till the clouds move, knowing He will appear.

2 CORINTHIANS 3:16

"But whenever anyone turns to the Lord, The veil is taken away."

If someone asked you if you were going to heaven when you died, what would you say? If someone asked you why you would go to heaven, what would you answer?

The Bible says, "For all have sinned and fall short of the glory of God." It also says, "The wages of sin is death." These verses make it seem like there is no hope for us. But God demonstrates His love in this, that while we are yet sinners, Christ died for us.

Great news for us!

The knowledge that Jesus died for you and to know He did it so you could be forgiven of your sins is a great moment. For by God's grace we are saved. We did nothing to deserve it. He did it all on the cross for us.

When you come to know the truth, then the veil is taken away, and you can really see what Jesus has done. Your life can change with this knowledge of Christ.

MY LIFE

Patty is my name, at least as a child that is what everyone called me. I was born in St. Louis County, Missouri, on January 30, 1946. Many birthdays with snow and ice came and went as I blew out the candles. When I was born, I already had a big brother named Danny. Yes, Danny and Patty, my mommy and daddy were proud to have the boy and girl they always wanted.

People who knew me as a child called me Patty; my family calls me Patty so, when I got married my husband called me Patty too. My given name is Patricia Ann, but Patty will do if you know me well. When I got out of school, Patty did not seem to be grown up enough for me, so I became Pat. If you got acquainted with me after the age of eighteen, you would know me as Pat. I know how long you have known me or how close you are to me by what you call me. A new preacher and his wife asked me what they should call me. I related this story to them and told them they could choose how to address me. Pastor called me Patty, the intimate name, and the pastor's wife called me Pat, the grown up name. But officially, if you want my signature, you would get Patricia.

As a child, I lived in a quaint little area of St. Louis called Melville. My house was built by my mom and dad and was on Lindbergh Blvd. We lived next door to all my dad's family. Right next door to us was my aunt Rosemary and uncle Willie and baby Lorrie. Next door to them were my grandma and grandpa in their big

Victorian house. On the other side of them were aunt Vernell and uncle Warren and my cousin Tommy. What a great place to grow up, with my family all in a row; I loved it.

My grandparents were truck farmers. They raised acres of vegetables and had orchards and patches of fruit. They had a stand at the market in downtown St. Louis, and every Saturday, they would head to market with a loaded truck full of vegetables. When Sunday came, they would set up a stand along the highway in front of their house to sell what was left. It was a great life of truck farming.

Grandma had a big kitchen with a wood stove for cooking. This was the room we all gathered in to talk and eat. Grandma always had food to serve to everyone who entered. They say my grandma had auburn hair, but I only knew her with gray hair. She always wore an apron with a bib on it. My Grandma was four foot and eleven inches tall and was round and soft, just right for a little girl to hug. I thought I was really lucky to have a grandma just my size.

One door in the kitchen led upstairs, and the other was the forbidden door ever since my brother Danny fell down those stairs and broke his arm when he jumped in front of me to save me from falling. He was my hero. It was always nice having a big brother to stand up for me and in front of me when I needed protection.

My grandmother's grandparents raised her. They came from Germany and lived on the land my grandparents farmed. My grandpa's parents lived up the road. Times were good, and my life was perfect living next door to the soft lady who could bake such great cookies for me. In the summer, my grandpa would make turtle soup and in the winter pickled herring. They were just good ole German folk.

Across the strawberry patch lived my best friend Barbara. I would eat strawberries all the way to Barbara's house and back during strawberry season. She was the preacher's daughter and lived next door to church. We loved to play dolls and would walk our dolls along the sidewalks of the cemetery pretending to take our dolls to town. I loved being with Barbara. She was the first friend I ever had, and I will always remember how I felt about my best friend and how we pretended and played.

My relatives founded the church across the strawberry patch, and we went every Sunday. I attended Sunday school and loved going to church because Barbara was there. The church was filled with aunts and uncles, my dad's cousins, and lots of school friends.

When I was eight years old, my dad bought a business in Cape Girardeau, Missouri, 125 miles away from my grandparents. I remember the day the moving van pulled up in front of my home. I felt like my world, as I knew it, would fall apart. No more warm cookies, no more strawberry patches, and no best friend named Barbara. My cousins would never come to my birthday parties any more, and Christmases at Grandmas were over. I cried all the way to my new home.

I would return to visit Grandma and Grandpa every summer for two weeks, and we would pick vegetables and go to market to sell them. We would leave at 4:00 a.m. and travel by rickety, old truck to the market. I would have a full day of eating raw veggies till I was sick; what fun! I would weigh the produce and bag it just like a clerk in a real store. It was a hard but fun day, because I was with my Grandma and Grandpa.

They would come for surprise visits to our new home. When I would see their little blue car in our driveway, as the bus pulled up from school to let me off, my heart would pound hard with excitement. I would run as fast as I could to be held in my Grandma's soft arms once more. I never knew my Grandpa snored so loudly, and when they came to visit us, we would all be up listening to him breath all night. But it was worth a few restless nights in exchange for all that love.

The first place I went on the first night in my new town, was Hanover skating rink run by the Lutheran Church members. The man my dad bought the business from was a member, and he loved to skate. They clamped the skates to my feet, and off I went to fall and fall and fall. Before the night was over, I did learn to skate a little. We did go back to try again, and each time I did get better. I thought I just might like this new town.

I met a new best friend on my street; her name was Lana, and she lived on the corner. We rode bikes together and spent many hours pretending to be the movie star Debbie Reynolds in love with Eddie Fisher, her movie star husband. We would ride down the hill in front of my house, with the wind blowing though our hair knowing we were beautiful just like Debbie Reynolds and truly in love with such a handsome man. Our paper dolls were of the Lennon Sisters, and we played for hours and hours with paper clothes, pretending we were singers on television. When my husband and I went to Branson for our wedding anniversary recently, we saw the Lennon Sisters, and I bought those same paper dolls I had as a child. This time, I will play paper dolls with my granddaughter.

I believe pretending, with nothing but our minds making up where we are, is the best way to play. Barbara and I were in streets of the city, not the cemetery. Lana and I were stars and beautiful and in love. We had all the feelings that we would need when we grew up, and that was good. We didn't need TV to entertain us, because we entertained ourselves by pretending.

I did move again but only a block away from Lana, and we were still best friends. We had all the dreams young girls dream of, marrying a movie star and living happily ever after. Lana and I were solid friends, even though we went to different schools. She went to Lutheran school, and I went to public school. We still spent as much time as we could with each other. We pretended and dreamed of our stardom.

Lana's daddy got ill with cancer. He could not taste or smell anymore, and he suffered a long time and then passed away. That was the first person I ever heard of that had cancer, but then Lana died from leukemia when she was fourteen years old, and I know she went to heaven. We may never understand the plans of God, and who will stay here and who will be called home, but we must trust that God knows what he is doing.

Friendships are important to young girls. Our friends know our inner secrets; we share our thoughts with them, and we share our dreams. As a young girl, I wanted to marry Eddie Fisher, and that was a secret that only Lana knew. All people need friends, best friends, to share our secrets and dreams with. Friends understand us and stand by us as we try to figure out our future. Lana knew when I married, I would marry a man with dark curly hair who looked just like Eddie Fisher.

The moving van had come once more and moved me away from Lana before she died. I was thirteen years old, and I had already lost two friends. That was very hard. Losses are not good for any one thirteen years old, no matter what the loss. My new home was across town, and Lana went to a different school. Would we ever see one another again? Would we still be best friends?

It was summer when we moved, and school was out so I couldn't even meet a friend at the bus stop. Around the corner, and down the next block was a girl named Nancy. She went to that Lutheran school too, so when school started, I never asked what grade she was in. When we were together, we would walk each other halfway home just to be together longer and talk. When we were apart, we would talk on the phone for hours. One Christmas, all I wanted was a white princess phone in my own room so I could talk to my friend, Nancy. We would share our thoughts on everything like boys, clothes, and life in general. I no longer dreamed of marrying Eddie Fisher, but boys were the main topic.

We would make scrapbooks, real scrapbooks. We would save any scrap that a boy we liked ever touched. We would save gum wrappers, soda cups, notes, and candy paper, anything that could tell about our life with boys, even though we did not date or even have a real boyfriend. We had dreams of dating, and dreams of boyfriends. We would laugh and giggle; we were best girlfriends.

Life in our new home was great; the house was a brand new split foyer with four levels. My dad's business was becoming successful; Mom and Dad bought a cabin on Kentucky Lake with a speedboat and a pontoon boat. My dad started flying planes, and he bought a new plane so we could fly off on vacation somewhere. He bought a car dealership to go with his truck dealership and built a new building to house both together. He was successful and times were good for our family. This is what we did on Sundays instead of church in our new town.

When school began, I thought Nancy and I would finally be going to the same school. The friendship had a strain when I found out she was only twelve but I was fourteen and going into high school; she would not be with me. I began dating a little when I was fifteen, and by the time I was sixteen, I had a steady boyfriend. He was six foot, four inches tall, and had dark, wavy hair. He had a cool car and dressed just like those guys you would see in the movie *Saturday Night Fever*, and looked like a tall Eddie Fisher.

Nancy and I saw less and less of one another after I went to high school. I had lots of friends in high school, but our activities had to fit around my boyfriend; he went to the University High School across town.

I was asked to join the sorority that was established at our school. I was still active in Girl Scouts till I graduated. I belonged to a lot of school clubs, and I sang in the choir. I only dated on weekends. I still roller-skated whenever I could; I can still remember how I felt circling the rink to music of my time. I wish I could still skate now, that feeling was awesome.

I graduated from high school in 1964. The Vietnam War was going on, and the Hippie movement had not yet come to our area. A lot of boys from my class were called to go to war. It was a scary time for everyone. The news was full of death, young boys losing their lives in service of our country.

I dated a lot of boys that died; I thought I caused it. Darrel was my first love. Our first date was at Nancy's Halloween party when he arrived with a blackened face like Al Jolson. No kissing went on that night and he did not die. Maybe it was my kisses that killed the others. Then I dated Gary. We talked on the phone a lot; he died in an accidental shooting after we stopped dating. Then I dated Dean, Gary's cousin, he looked just like Eddie Fisher too. He died later from an illness. I dated Lyman; he gave me a diamond, and we planned to marry. We broke up before the wedding, and he died in a truck crash at work years later. I dated two farmers, Arnold and Gib. I dated them both at the same time. I did choose Gib, and Arnold and I broke up; Arnold died in a car crash a week later. Gib and I married, but he never left me for fear of the kiss of death.

I was sheltered growing up, never trying things that would get me into trouble. I never drank, smoked, or used drugs, although drugs were not so common in my hometown. We were all pretty good kids back then. There were a few guys in leather jackets that smoked and hung around together, we called them Hoods, but I didn't hang with them. Girls were not allowed to come to school pregnant, they were sent away to have their babies. If you got pregnant, you kept the baby or sent it away to be adopted; no other choice was given. So as a result, there were very fewer pregnancies in high school. Not everyone had sex, because we had to be responsible for our actions.

I was always more mature than other girls at my age. I remember when I was ten and eleven going to town on the city bus shopping by myself. When I was sixteen years old, my mom and dad had another son named David. I was like a third parent to him and loved giving him bottles and playing mommy.

When David was four months old, my mom and dad went on a business trip to Georgia. They left me in charge of the baby. David was still on formula and wore cloth diapers. I would make the formula and wash the diapers and take care of the house. I was very responsible for a sixteen-year-old. One year, Mom and Dad took me out of school to go on vacation with them to take care of the baby. I loved my new brother. My life growing up was full of warm fuzzy feelings and love. I matured and dreamed of the future and old age seemed so far away. I lived my life fully as a child.

At the end of high school on prom night, my boyfriend, Lyman, asked me to marry him. Of course I said yes, and we began planning our wedding for October 20, 1964. I bought the dress and ordered the invitations. We rented a little house, and I started painting it when the date got closer. I went out and bought his ring and ordered the cake. The plans were made, and the dates were set, and things were on schedule. My parents did not like my choice of a husband. I guess because he didn't work much and bought the engagement ring with unemployment checks.

On August 29, 1964, my boyfriend, Lyman, decided to go out with a former girlfriend for one last fling, and I broke up with him. I was so devastated; my only real love had left me for another. The wonderful man who looked like Eddie Fisher (but taller) left me.

I was young and brokenhearted. Oh, I believed in God, so I prayed to God to send me a wonderful man to love me and never leave me. I believed God loved me, and He would answer my prayers, so I waited for the answer.

In January, Gib asked me out on a date and stole my heart. He was different from all the other boys I had dated. He was twenty-three and was a good ole farm boy from a town thirty miles away called Perryville. He would drive thirty miles to pick me up on our date, and we would go back to Perryville. Then he would drive me back home only to return to Perryville for the night.

After seven months of driving back and forth, Gib asked me to marry him on August 29, 1965, one year to the day after the engagement breakup with Lyman. We never talked about marriage.

I was shocked when he handed me the diamond ring. It was just like our life together would always be. We would never really talk about the big things in our life; we just knew they were right to do.

God answered my prayers the night I asked him for the man of my dreams. Gib was five feet four inches tall; he had blond, wavy hair and was cute. He was no Eddie Fisher! We were married on November 20, 1965. He was a hard worker and a family man. But most importantly, he was a religious man who never missed church. For the first time in my life, church was a big part of it. I let God choose, and He gave me the best. The years to come would be years I would need a husband like Gib, and God knew it.

Gib had enough money saved to buy us a house trailer, and we parked it in a little trailer park in Cape Girardeau, Missouri. David, my little brother, was three years old and thought he was moving in with us. He was very upset to find out he had to stay with our mom and dad. He did come to stay with us a lot; he called the extra bedroom his.

It was a time of love and happiness. Our first Christmas tree was decorated with all our wedding bows. I was nineteen years old, and I thank God He sent me a grown up who would take care of me. I thought I was ready to be a wife, but that is a big job, and I had to grow into it. So we lived in our little home and loved one another.

After two years, we moved our trailer to my parents' new farm. They had plenty of land, and we put our cute little home next to the creek. I could watch the animals at the barn across the creek. I was always a tomboy at heart, and I would shoot snakes off the creek bank. Gib fit right in, being from the country, he loved to garden and fix fence and he, with my dad, built barns and raised cattle together. Gib would mow the pasture and feed the cattle every night. My dad and he were great friends.

Our first son was born while we lived on the farm in our little trailer. We named him Scott Carroll, the *Carroll* after my dad. He was beautiful. What joy this baby brought to us. I thanked God for the perfect little son he gave me. He had strawberry blond hair and was so little and cute. There is no better feeling on this earth, as the feeling you get looking at what you created with the one you love. I knew that God knitted him together in my womb. I truly do not understand how someone could harm a child. My son was so innocent, so needy. Our family had begun.

I worked at my dad's truck sales until I was ready to have the baby, and never worked full time again. Women were going to work all around me, but I really wanted to stay home and raise my son. It wasn't the thing to do back then, but I am thankful now I stayed home because of how short the time is. The children in our home would be gone to a place of their own very shortly. It was the best decision I made in my life, to have less and give more time to my family. We could have had an easier life with more money, but my children would benefit more with me at home teaching them values only a mom can teach. We made the decision for me to be their mom full time.

We moved to our first home when Scott was one. It was a small house a couple miles down the road from my parents. We had nine acres of land, a little screened-in porch, and the house was like our little dream house with white fencing around it. We would live here four years.

We had a large garden and I canned everything I could get my hands on. One year, I canned 300 quarts of fruits and vegetables to help with our finances. I also cut everyone's hair just to save a dollar. I knew if I was to be successful at being a mom, I needed to cut back on everything. We raised calves on the bottle and sold them at the sale barn. Gib farmed on the side and cut wood to sell. It was a good life with supper on the table every night and the family all together.

Our second son was named Timothy Christian, *Christian* after Gib's dad. He was the happiest baby I ever saw. He smiled the first time I laid eyes on him. I loved those boys more than anything on this earth, and they would always be part of my heart. To this day, my boys bring me nothing but joy. They never made me sad or sorry, only happy and proud that they were my sons.

Life in the country was good. We had two German shepherd dogs named Bert and Ernie. The boys would run with their dogs by their sides. We had a pony named Ticky, and he would graze in the back yard while the boys played. When Scott turned five he had a birthday party with pony rides.

Living in the country with money tight and two small boys, I was very lonely and my girlfriend Linda, who was a friend in grade school, became my phone buddy. She moved back to town after being gone for years. We would talk on the phone for hours. As stay at home moms we needed adult conversation. We would solve the problems of the world during the boys' naptime. She had two small boys too, and we would discuss the raising of boys, which was challenging.

I would spend a lot of time at my mom's pool in the summers swimming with the boys. We really enjoyed our life in the country. Although we were only in the country four years, it seemed like the days were long with plenty of time to do the things we wanted to do. It seems like only yesterday we were sitting on our screened in porch.

In my own life, I look back at the choices I have had to make to be happy. At the age of twenty-two, I was told after the birth of my first child not to have any more; too many complications. This made me very confused and very sad thinking I could have no more children. As a woman, I wanted more children. I guess we are just made to long for babies. I agonized over what the doctor said, and then decided to have one more no matter what the cost. For most of the nine months, I had a lot of complications, just as the doctor said I would. I was housebound, and the baby was two weeks late. The labor was long and the delivery life threatening. I had surgery six months after delivery to repair the damage done during the birth. Then the doctor repeated, "Absolutely no more children!"

I had a choice to either be sad or love the two boys God had given me. I was blessed to have two, instead of one child. I made a choice to be happy with what I had and not dwell on what I did not have. My boys were healthy, and so was I. God brought me through the hard pregnancy and delivery. I realized God's presence in my life, and He carried me through.

Scott was such an active boy; his antics often made me gasp. Scott had no fear! He was a climber, and it all started when he was an infant. The first time I knew he was a climber he was about nine months old. He could stand with help but could not walk. We lived in our trailer, and his room was small. The built-in dresser was about a foot and a half away from the bed. When I walked into the room he was sitting on the dresser! I do not know how he got there, but he climbed out of bed and across the span. I breathed in!

Scotty couldn't walk but could climb on the couch and to the back of it and look out the window. He would scoot a chair to the kitchen cabinets and climb on them when I wasn't looking. I was afraid to leave him alone in the room. When we moved into our country home, because it was a bigger area, I would put all the kitchen chairs on top of the table and put up two gates, before we could begin our day together.

When Scotty was about two, he had a little tractor that had no pedals; he just walked with it between his legs. Gib was up on the hill next to our home planting the garden. Scotty saw his daddy up there and began his long trek up the hill dragging the tractor. He had to climb over or under the board plank fence. When I looked out, he was on top of the hill ready to ride his little tractor down the hill into a concrete ditch. I gave out a terrified scream saying, "Stop," and he let go of the tractor, and it came clamoring down the hill without him and crashed into the concrete at the bottom of the hill. I breathed in!

On another climbing adventure, Scotty climbed over two fences onto the back roof of our garage. This level was in the ground and the front was normal; he walked over the roof and down the other side. He fell off the roof into a bunch of surprise lilies in the spring. Gib came in to get barbecue sauce for the meat on the grill; it only took a minute out of sight to breathe in.

When Scotty was almost three, I was pregnant with Timmy and was at the beauty shop under the dryer; Scotty was sitting by my feet. A lady entered the shop, and in a flash Scotty jumped up, ran out the door, between two cars, and out into the busy street. Once again, I screamed, "Stop," and he stopped. I breathed in! When Timmy arrived, Scotty had a playmate, and he did not have to be so adventurous. Scotty was a good big brother most of the time. Scotty had to share everything when his brother arrived. He had to share his toys, his room, and his mom and dad. Timmy wasn't an only child until he was eighteen when Scott moved out.

Timmy was a ten-pound bundle of joy. He was a baby with a smile on his face and a very pleasant personality. Timmy always followed Scott's lead and he loved it. Timmy only got into trouble if Scott did and he followed. The boys only had a few scuffs in their lives, because they were best friends and brothers.

I put Timmy in a playpen when he was a baby, so Scotty wouldn't try to help me too much. Timmy would sit in his playpen and play. He loved it and never climbed out or even tried to. I never breathed in with Timmy. He was not adventurous; he was a lap sitter, and he would sit on anyone's lap if they would let him. My dad said to my mom, "Anne, I think you like Timmy better than Scotty because you are always holding him." Mom said, "No, I don't. He keeps backing up to me to be held."

When Timmy was three years old, one night he had a tummy ache. We put him in our bed and watched him all night. At five in the morning he had such a pain, his little body left the bed and he screamed. I called the doctor, and he told me to bring him in at eight. He had a fever and was in pain. The doctor explained to me he needed exploratory surgery to find out what was wrong. He said, "We may open him up and find nothing and sew him right back up, but we need to find out what's wrong because it could be serious."

At the age of three, my youngest son underwent major surgery to remove part of his colon. As I sat in the waiting room hour after hour, I chose not to be sad, for God was with us, and He would carry us through this trauma. My baby was close to death; he would never be the same, and all kinds of fear began to fill my thoughts. I made a choice that day to be happy and not let fear rule over me. I thank God I was saved the year before, and I had God to watch over me.

The surgery took hours, and we just waited. Grandma and Grandpa were with Scotty, so they sent flowers to Timmy's room, and we waited. After four hours, the nurse came in and told us Timmy was in intensive care, and the doctor would tell us what he found. She handed us the flowers and wheeled Timmy's empty bed down the hallway toward intensive care. The doctor found gangrene of the colon and removed one third of the large intestine and nine inches of the small and the valve between them. My little boy had a large incision down his little tummy. The pathologist took pictures of it and wrote a paper about it, for this was only found in older people and never in babies.

Timmy was in intensive care for a week with all the very sick adults in the hospital; there was not a pediatric ICU at that time. The nurse told us we could only visit ten minutes every other hour. We could not visit after eight in the evening and not before eight in the morning, but we could call at 7:00 a.m. to see how he did during the night. We went home and slept; it was thirty-six hours since my eyes had been closed in sleep.

At 7:00 a.m. the next morning, I called, and I could hear Timmy screaming in the background. They said, "Mrs. Renner, you can come up and stay with him if you want." So I rushed to the hospital.

When I arrived, he was still screaming; I knew why he was screaming the moment I looked at him. The thumb he always sucked was strapped to a board that kept it still for the IV. I told him he could suck the other thumb, and I put it into his mouth. I wiped the tears from his wet little face and rubbed my fingers through his hair, and he calmed down. I stayed at the hospital twenty hours a day, only sleeping four hours at a time when Gib could relieve me in the evenings.

My mom and dad took care of Scotty, so we didn't have to worry about him. We told Scotty about his brother's new zipper on his tummy, and my brother David drew a zipper on Scotty's tummy for our welcome home. Timmy loved his brother's big red zipper just like his.

When I look back at that time now, I saw how God was watching over us. He was giving us all we needed to withstand this trying time in our lives. God saved my child from death, and I was going to rejoice and be happy he was alive.

When Timmy was four years old, nine months after the surgery, on Christmas Eve, he got a tummy ache. I called the doctor. We were sent right to the hospital and checked in. We were there Christmas Eve, Christmas Day, and came home the day after. Timmy had the flu! I was glad to be there in a safe place in case it all happened again. We had Christmas when we got home, and Santa brought Timmy a big red two-wheel bike.

When the boys were two and five years old, we had moved to the city. I watched the boys grow up in a neighborhood full of boys. Gib was farming, and so we played. I taught the boys how to hit a ball, ride a bike, shoot a gun, swim, and just how to pretend like children do.

Raising boys was great fun, since I was a tomboy myself. I was the only girl in a neighborhood of boys when I was young, so I learned to do things boys liked to do. As a mother, I found myself at every ball game. I was the sideline cheerleader for the boys. They played soccer, football, baseball, and basketball. I spent a lot of time on the bleachers watching them play ball.

One day the neighbors where trying to catch a non-poisonous snake in their yard. Timmy wanted to take this snake to show and tell at school. So being a tomboy myself, I went over to catch the snake and put it in a jar. Seemed like a simple task to me. My brother always had snakes at home, and I helped him with them, so as I reached down for the snake, it bit me! Then my son wanted me to go to show and tell because a mom with snakebite was much, much better than any old snake in a jar.

I helped as a room mother for the school parties, baking cupcakes and attending all the parties. I was the Cub Scout leader for the boys' dens. I wore that cute yellow shirt that all the den mothers wore. When it was time for Timmy's den to become Boy Scouts and have a man lead the group, no man came forward. They asked me if I would become the leader. Women were never Boy Scout leaders at that time! I agreed to lead the boys, so the den could continue. This level of scouting is to let the fathers teach the boys how to camp, hike, hunt, fish—you know, men things. No fathers would do this and it was up to me to teach their sons to be men.

One of the gifts God gave me is the gift of organization. My first outing with the new troup was to plan a father son campout. We all would go to my parent's farm and camp together for the weekend. No one knew what I had planned. I had it so organized that the boys could earn a merit badge by hiking with one of the fathers in the early morning hours. Another father took them fishing to earn a badge. We had campfires with skits and Indian dancing. They cooked over the fire, camped in tents, gathered rocks for the rock collections, and did some first aid. The boys earned a lot of badges that weekend while I sat in the motor home, with electricity, air-conditioning, and a real bed. I really didn't camp with them; I just organized the event. The men got the vision as to what the Boy Scouts were about, and there was a father to replace me right away.

I remember one summer, the boys had some plywood that Gib didn't want and built a fort in the back yard with windows, a door, and a roof. They played all summer in that fort. The next summer they took the same wood and built a tree house on the top of the jungle gym; it had windows and they played all summer in the tree house. The next summer that wood became a soapbox car with wheels and a steering system and a window on the hood of the car. The next summer the wood became ramps for bike jumping. The next summer they dug a big hole in the ground for a hideout, and the wood became the trap door. This underground hideout took most of July to dig. It was equipped with electricity and carpet. It was a wonderful place to spend a hot, dry summer day. All was well until the big rain came, and the hideout became an in-ground swimming pool.

The boys had a great time playing. They were always building or planning to build something. Scott was the leader and Tim the follower, and they liked it that way. Always planning and playing together, they were best friends and still are.

They got involved with remote control cars as teenagers, and this took the place of dating girls, and I was glad. They had a trunk with "Renner Racing Team" on it. They were a great team. Tim was the driver of the remote car, and Scott the builder, mechanic ,and manager. We would take them all over to race, and when they were at home, they would spend time at the hobby shop buying or selling racecars. When they got older, they bought dune buggies and started racing and riding them. The toys just got bigger harmless fun.

We were always involved in our boys' lives, and it went too fast. It is unbelievable that Scott and Tim have been gone from home over twenty years now. We think there is a lot of time, but it is fleeting. I can't believe the boys are in their forties now.

God was with us all throughout our lives and kept us all safe and secure. We did not have much money as the boys were growing up, but we had a lot of love in our house. The boys went to the same Lutheran School my friends Lana and Nancy attended. And they learned to know Jesus.

I never regret being a full time mom because I look back now and see how time has flown by, and I wouldn't want to have missed a minute of life with my boys. They are my heart.

The greatest hope I have for my sons is to fall in love with a woman who will make them happy for the rest of their lives. I raised the boys to be great husbands; they could cook, clean, and do the laundry. They were not chauvinistic or mean. I knew they would love their wives and be faithful to them forever. What more could a daughter-in-law want? Now I would pray that God would send them someone to love forever.

The biggest fear I have is that the boys would not marry or find someone to love. Gib and I are in love and our relationship is great. It would be such heartache if the boys did not have love in their lives. It would be sheer pain to live in love while watching your child live without someone to hold and kiss.

Scott dated Christie. She stayed in Cape after graduation from Southeast Missouri State University and was working there when they met. He asked her out on February 24th, and she accepted. Christie loved Scott and she showed her love for him to everyone. On February 24th, one year later, they married.

Tim met Jennifer while she was still in college at SEMO. She was a hard working gal going to college and working part-time. She loved to have fun, and they laughed together; she made Tim very happy. Tim asked Jennifer to marry him just before her senior year of college.

The weddings were sixty-three days apart; that was a good year with two new daughters-in-laws in one year. I like to call them daughters-in-love because of how happy both the boys were, and still are. You can tell that God made the union between them because of how perfectly they fit together. I could not have picked better women for my sons. When you trust God with the details, all is well.

Now I have 3 wonderful grandchildren: Jourdan, Cole, and Shelby. They are the joy of my heart. I love being a grandmother. Being part of a family is important to me, and I have a good one.

LUKE 3:16

"I baptize you with water. But one more powerful than I will come, the thongs of whose sandals I am not worthy to untie. He will baptize you with the Holy Spirit and with fire."

John was baptizing people throughout the land. John knew there would be one sent straight from God to baptize people with the Holy Spirit and fire. John lived in expectation of the future one to come, the one sent by God. He had hope for the future. He knew the prophecy of the one to come that would bring the Holy Spirit to the people.

We know the promises of God that Jesus will return and those in Christ will raise to dwell with the King forever. Yet, we do not live in expectation of the one to come, the one who will be King of Kings and Lord of Lords.

Reverence Jesus Christ, and humble yourselves before Him. Make Him Lord of you life and bow before Him. The King is coming.

BIG CHANGES

When I was twelve, my Grandma, Nana, my mom's mother, moved from Nashville to live with us for a few years before finding her own place in town. She never wanted to be called grandma, so I called her Nana, even though I really wanted her to be my grandma. Her husband ran off with the neighbor lady and Nana got a divorce and I never saw Bubby, my grandpa, again. Nana wasn't as old looking as my other grandma. She dated and danced and worked at a department store in town. She wrote poems and painted and she took me to church with her. When my family moved to Cape Girardeau, Missouri we went to church for a year or so, then stopped going to church so church was not a big part of my life. As I think back now, I am very grateful to Nana for taking me to church with her again when I was twelve. It was just the beginning of a great walk I would take someday with my Lord.

After Nana moved out, I walked to the little Baptist Church four blocks away and went with a girlfriend from school named Brenda. I went there Sunday morning and Sunday night and then again on Wednesdays. When I dated Lyman, a Methodist boy, I went to church for about four years with him off and on. I was always searching for a home church; I wanted to know God.

While Gib and I lived in the country, we didn't attend church much. The church we wanted to go to would not let us go there when we moved, it was the wrong diocese. We had to go to a church closer to where we lived. As a result, we attended less and less. We really wanted to go to church, but felt we had none of our own. One day, we passed a neighborhood church on a Sunday morning and all our neighbors were standing outside the church talking to one another. This church was of a different denomination than the one we belonged to, but we did know the people. We decided to attend the next week.

The name of the church was Hanover Lutheran Church. It was the church with the skating rink I went to the first night in Cape Girardeau. Who knew that sixteen years after skating that night, I would be back at that skating rink? God knows our every move; he knows our beginning and our ending, he knows our coming and our going. He knew I would end up at this very church.

The sun was bright the day we went to Hanover for the first time. The people inside were very friendly. We took our seats and opened the hymnal to sing. I thought, *what a nice church. Maybe we could attend church here on Sundays; maybe this could be our church home.* Great and mighty things were about to happen to my husband and me that day. This would prove to be the best day of our lives. This would be the day that changed me forever. It seemed like God drew me to this church from the first day I was in my new town after crying all the way there.

Then the pastor began his sermon, which was on the farmer sowing seed in the ground. This topic was dear to my husband's heart, and he could understand what the pastor was talking about with the rocky ground where the seed could not take hold, and how the good ground was the best to help the seed to grow. This was describing our love for God. We need to be the good ground so the seed of God's word can grow within us. My husband and I came to know God in an intimate way that day sitting together in the pew of our new church. I heard the pastor say we were sinners; he said,

All have sinned and fall short of the glory of God.

Romans 3:23

I knew I was a sinner, and I knew I had fallen short. I just wanted to be good enough for God to love me. The pastor said we were all sinners, even him, and I knew I was in the right place among the sinners who felt the way I did.

Then the pastor read another verse from the Bible,

> For the wages of sin is death, but the gift of God is eternal life in Jesus Christ our Lord.
>
> Romans 6:23

I knew I didn't please God the way I was and God was offering me a free gift of eternal life, so I could live with Him forever. This was what I had been looking for my whole life, a way to live in God's presence forever and ever.

Then the pastor gave me the answer I needed; he read the word of God, which said,

> … but God demonstrates his own love for us in this: While we were still sinners, Christ died for us.
>
> Romans 5:8

While I was still a sinner, Jesus Christ died for me. I didn't have to do a thing, Christ did it all for me, while I was still a sinner; He was the one who would change me.

God sent His only son, Jesus, to earth to die on a cross for my sin. He was raised from the dead, and He now lives. What good news it was for me that day, the day I came to believe. Years later, when Gib and I were talking about when we were saved, I related this time as the time God saved me. Gib related the same time, same day, and same sermon, as the day God saved him too. This was the greatest day for both of us; the day we were saved side-by-side forever.

My life began to change that day. Oh, not drastically, but slowly over the years. It took five years to get to know God intimately and personally. Now I wanted to live for Him every day, not just on weekends for an hour on Sunday, but live for Him every moment of every day. Now He was first in my life. I was learning to give up the things in my life that were not God pleasing and learning to lean on Him and trust Him with my life. God wanted to use me, and I was being pruned.

I was still a sinner, although I did not want to be. I would still sin, but my heart was not a heart that loved sinning anymore. My heart was a heart for God now. When I would sin now, I would be repentant and longed to please God and was so sorry for my sin. Even the smallest of sin made me sad that I would dishonor God in such a way. But I seemed to keep on sinning. I thank God that He has given me a way out. Jesus is the way and when I do sin, Jesus covers me. He died so I could live forgiven and free.

Every day, I learn a new lesson from God, but I have to look for God's involvement in my life every day. He is always there when I seek Him. Sometimes, God teaches me through Bible studies I attend, or when I read from His word alone at home. God teaches me through a sermon, devotions I read, or Christian TV shows I watch. He is a great teacher, and I learn from Him daily.

We are examples to others, so they see God glorified through us. His lesson one day began in Sunday school, when the teacher spoke on how God wants us to act. We really fall short of what He expects, so we need His forgiveness all the time. I seem to be sorry all the time when I read God's word, because I am a sinner. I am like Paul in the Bible, the good I want to do, I can't, and what I truly don't want to do, this is what I do.

In class, we spoke about being doers of the Word, not just listeners. We talked about faith and how the good deeds we do are the result of that faith. We are an example to others every moment of the day. Boy, what a responsibility. People were watching me to see how I reacted; was I angry, upset, jealous, envious, or weak? Or was I kind, humble, joyful, patient, and loving? Did I trust God and His promises to me?

I prayed before the sermon to ask for wisdom. The sermon that day was moving and stirred my heart. It was about fear binding me, and how I could overcome fear by trusting God. The pastor spoke about giving tithes, time, and service to God, and how we should no longer be bound by fear and should release it to God.

I had never realized how closely others watch me when I say I am a Christian. They are looking for answers to fear and life's challenges, and God is the answer. To grow strong and be a good example, I need to go to church often, because I am not righteous, and I need a Savior to forgive me too. I need to worship God, the only one who really loves me unconditionally. I need the fellowship of other believers all the time. I need to hear how God really loves me and thinks I am precious to Him. When I have all this, others can watch me to see a strong Christian who has all her trust in the Lord and does not fear. I am a good example at these times.

I realized that day that God had been providing for me all my life. He gave me just what I needed, just when I needed it. He removed my fear and saved my life. He gave me friends when I cried out and someone to love me when I prayed. He blessed me with beautiful boys who would never disappoint me. How could I ever repay such a great God who loved me so much? God expected no payment, but I loved Him so much, I wanted to give something back out of love in return.

God was in my life, even when I didn't know it. When Gib and I first married, we bought a house trailer and lived in it four years. One day, we went to visit one of the neighbors down the road. We loved their home, with the white picket fence and the screened in porch, it was a so cute. We asked them if they wanted to sell it; they said, "No." Nine months later they came to us and offered us their house for a great price, and we bought it. We sold our trailer for almost what we paid for it, and we were now happy homeowners. We lived there four years. God was in control of it all.

Then God gave us a brand new home to live in. We never planned to move again, but one day Gib asked me to go to town and look at houses to see what they cost. We had nine acres and could build one day on some of it or just add a room to our present home if building costs were out of our budget. So, I took the boys and my mom to town and went with a realtor to look at new homes. I found two that would meet our need if we did not build. One was a split foyer, and one was a ranch; this gave different styles for Gib to look at.

That evening, we went to meet the realtor once more, just to show Gib the two houses. We were not in the market to buy a new home, especially in town, when we had nine acres out in the country with our cattle, pony, tractors, and big garden. We looked at the split foyer and it was nice. Then we looked at the ranch, but it was not quite complete. There was a board with the carpet and counter top samples on it. The realtor said we could pick out our own colors if we bought it. When the man stopped talking, Gib looked at me and said, "Let's buy it." I said, "Ok," and that was it. We signed the papers, gave the realtor a $500.00 earnest money postdated check, and went home.

We were more surprised than anyone because of what we did, and we were in shock. We just bought a home, and we already had one. There was not $500.00 in our checking account or savings account either. But remember, I was trusting God now. I know things are easy when God is in control. This was God's way to show us His faithfulness.

The next day, I went to the bank and borrowed $500.00 to cover the check we wrote. Then I bought a house for sale ad in the newspaper and a sign for the yard. The newspaper ran the ad on Monday, and we sold the house by ourselves on Wednesday. The first people who bought it could not get a loan at the bank, and on Saturday, another couple came to sign papers to buy our home, while more buyers sat in the driveway waiting to see if these second people really bought it.

I did get to choose the inside colors of our new home: the carpet, wall color, wallpaper, drapes, counter tops, and appliances. It was like a dream. I was in a new home, and we had enough money left from the sale of our house to buy new furniture. Our home was complete, and we knew it was truly a gift from God.

God loved us and gave us the desires of our hearts. We didn't even know what that desire was, but looking back, I see that this was the right move for us. We have been in this home since 1973. God is good. The boys were raised here, and we never regretted moving. A lot of people think and talk and wish for years before they get a new home. We never even thought about a new home in town, not even once. We had the money to buy a new home and never had a savings account. We didn't have enough furniture to fill our new home. We went from a four-room, one-bath home to an eight-room, two-and-a-half-bath home. God provided us with enough furniture to fill every room. I knew God loved us and was doing what was good for us. We needed to recognize that this was His gift to us. We needed to give Him first place in our lives.

I learned a lot the first five years of my walk with the Lord. I learned that there is nothing that goes on in my life that God is not involved in, and that I should always learn something from Him every day. He is in control of all things, even the smallest detail. I learned that I should trust Him without question, because He wants only good for me. I can learn from everything that comes my way, because I look for God in it.

My husband never lived in town before, but there he was in a subdivision. It was where we needed to be with two boys who would be in sports and lots of activities. Our neighborhood was full of boys to play with. God was in control of our lives all the time, even when we did not realize it.

ACTS 3:16

"By Faith in the name of Jesus, this man whom you
see and know was made strong. It is Jesus' name and
the faith that comes through him that has given this
complete healing to him, as you can all see."

Peter prayed and the crippled beggar was healed and all were
amazed. Peter had faith in Jesus and by His name the beggar was
healed. There is power in the name of Jesus. The beggar had great
faith in Jesus and he was healed. Your faith will make you strong.
The beggar was made strong by his faith in Jesus. We too can call
upon His name and become strong. If you need healing of your
body, soul, or spirit have the faith like the beggar and you will be
healed. Know who holds the power to heal: Jesus. We pray and He
heals. Call upon the name of Jesus the healer for all your needs.

GOOD HEALTH, BAD HEALTH

At the age of eighteen, my health started downhill. I got very sick and went to the doctor with a sore throat. He gave me penicillin, and I reacted to it. I was never sick before, and the reaction to the medication was complicated because I was baby-sitting my two-year-old brother while my parents were on a business trip to Georgia. My hands and feet and every joint in my body were swollen. I couldn't walk or crawl; I could only scoot on my butt to get around. I had to call one girlfriend to come to take care of my brother and another girlfriend to come and take care of me. I was never allergic to anything before.

By the time I was twenty-five years old, I had very bad allergies. I went to the doctor to get tested to see just what made me allergic. I had 150 skin tests done and had bad reactions to all but six. I was not allergic to fish, oats, oranges, nuts, dogs, and kapok (that's stuffing for pillows); all the rest of the tests were bad. I began allergy shots once a week for ten years. I still have some allergies, but after the age of sixty, the allergies got better.

The day of the allergy tests, the doctor asked me if I smoked, and I denied it. Then he said my allergies were so bad I would die by the age of thirty if I did. I never smoked again. When my 30th birthday arrived, I was very relieved I was not dying as the doctor predicted, and I was glad I had quit smoking. I felt as if a large burden was lifted off of me when that day came and went.

The winter of 1977, Mom and Dad and our family went to Florida, in my parent's motor home. The morning we left Florida the temperature was in the high eighties, and I walked on the beaches of St. Petersburg; it was lovely. Then we began our trip back home. When we reached Chattanooga, Tennessee, there were ice storms, but we arrived home safely. The next morning, I was downstairs doing laundry, and I couldn't get up the stairs. At thirty-one years of age, and after days of doctor's visits and tests, I was diagnosed with one of the forty forms of muscular dystrophy (inflammation of the muscles). The muscles would only bother me if I used them, and there was pain everywhere there was a muscle. I couldn't get around my own home.

I was going to the beauty shop once a week to get my hair done, and Della, the lady just before me, had fallen at work. She too was going through test after test to find out why she was still in pain after her fall. Each week we would get together at the beauty shop and compare notes.

That same week, the doctor found my chronic illness, Della found out she had bone cancer, a terminal disease. Della would die and I would live. I decided to live life fully for the Lord because He let me stay here and did not call me home like Della.

I was going to be in pain for the rest of my life. How was I going to handle this new challenge?

When I was thirty-one years old, my life was taken away. Maybe the devil took it, or maybe it was just my own sin; maybe, like Job, it was for the testing of my faith. I don't know. It doesn't really matter; all I know is my health was stolen from me.

When you ask someone what is the most important thing in their life, it would probably be their health. My health was ripped away overnight, my boys were only eight and five years old. They had half a mom; Gib, my husband, had half a wife; and I was half a person.

When illness strikes you, your friends abandon you rapidly. They speak cordially but really don't want to hear about you, so I was all alone facing the rest of my life. My friends did not call anymore. I didn't talk about my illness because it turned people off. No one wants to hear about your strife and pain. So I cried in silence.

My parents, husband, and children had to learn to live with this illness too. We did not speak of the illness, we just began to cope. The boys took on more responsibilities than other boys their age. My husband took on the job of caretaker of his wife, who physically was almost useless. My parents had a lot of sadness because they could not fix it. No one knew the future.

I didn't cry in front of anyone, I was brave in public, but in private I cried out to God for my strength to endure. I tried not to complain about the pain and did the best I could do every day. I tried to focus my mind on other things and not on myself. The part of my life I did not like was suffering alone. No one really knew of the true suffering in my life alone at night, I was up till the wee hours in the morning because the pain kept me awake.

I needed to turn to God. He was going to walk with me and lead me through the turmoil and the pain. I could no longer play with the boys; I could only watch them play. I could hardly do the everyday chores at home. I had a lot of bad days and nights sitting in pain. I was overwhelmed by it. There was so much pain in my life; I couldn't remember what it was like to be without it.

Somewhere in my body, at all times, there is pain. Throbbing, uncontrollable, consuming pain is now my old friend. I learned to live with the pain and adjust my life. There is a constant awareness of intense suffering. Through years watching my two boys grow up, missing out on the best years of their lives. I could not be the mother I truly wanted to be.

There were days when I didn't want to get out of bed, but I did. There were days when I didn't want to leave the house, but I did. I could not have made it without God by my side to give me strength. I began reading the Bible and went to a lot of Bible studies. I got a relationship with Jesus, my Savior. I was getting well on the inside and sick on the outside. That is a lot better than being well on the outside and spiritually sick on the inside.

I did not carry laundry baskets, or heavy things, because of the muscles. The saddest part for me was that I did not carry my grandchildren either. I could put their little butts on the table and cradle them in my arms. I could not baby-sit for them alone until they could crawl into my lap by themselves.

I didn't know I could not hold them until the first night I was with my first grandchild, Jourdan, and she was only a few days old when I held her in my arms and walked around the room rocking and loving her. I was at my mom's house in the country. When the evening was over, and I got into the car to go home, I got halfway home and the pain set in. I stopped the car because the pain was so bad. I couldn't drive anymore. Someone I knew stopped to see if I was all right, and I said they should call Gib. He came and took me home. The husband God sent saved me more than once in my life from all the pain.

In my family, we all learned to live with my illness. Gib would drop me off at doors so I didn't have to walk because I couldn't without pain. I couldn't lift a lot, so someone else would do it. And on rainy days, I might lie in bed all day. But we never talked about it much; we just lived with it. The illness was like having a big pink elephant in the room, but no one mentioned it was there; we all pretended it was not.

I spoke of the pain only to God, complaining and crying only to Him. The Holy Spirit that God gave me came alive in me to give me comfort. When I just couldn't stand the agony any more, God would release it from me by making me content and at peace in my heart and mind. I am not content without God in my life. My life is full because of Jesus Christ; I am never alone, and He is my new friend. He is all I need.

No one asks and really wants to know how I feel. No person can feed my soul or hear my silent cries like my Lord. No one in this world really knows how bad it is for me. Only one person really cares, and that is Jesus. When times are bad, he sends my boys or family to my rescue, to love me through the bad times.

One day Scott called. I asked him why he called and he couldn't remember, he said I was just on his mind. So we chatted, and I told him I loved him and he responded with, "I love you too, Mom." My tears stopped and pain eased some, God had sent me help. Scott did not know I had been crying, and God protected me from my tears of self-pity that always make the pain worse.

I will go on with the help of the Lord. I am worth nothing without my Lord, He empowers me to look strong, speak strong, and be strong in Him. One day God will take away my thorn and I will thank Him. The pain is constant, and at times I will cry. I will live a life that honors God. Where are my friends? Jesus is my friend. Who cares about me? Jesus cared enough to die for me. Jesus can hear the silent cries, and I am never alone.

I fell a lot when I was younger with the muscle disease. I would fall down steps a lot but always held on to the railings and just rip the muscles in my arms, and I injured my neck. I had a new pain in the neck. I learned not to carry groceries by the bag, so I would bring in my groceries a few things at a time all by myself. One day, my mom and I were fishing, and I fell in the boat. I didn't get hurt, I thought, but the next day I couldn't stand the pain from the injured nerve in my upper back. I could not sit down or lay down. I could only stand. I put a bed in the family room to spend my nights there. After six months the pain finally left.

Once I carried too many heavy boxes. Everyone has lifted things they should have left for a pack mule; I should have walked away. But I just needed to move the boxes a little bit. I thought, *I wouldn't be moving them far.* I'll lift them quickly and set them down fast. I got back pain that started as a mild, persistent lower back pain. I thought it would go away. So I continued living with it. After a month it grew worse every day. I sat more and rested my back, hoping this would cure it.

The pain started to run down my leg. The pain was fierce and intense. I could not control it; relief was not easy to find. The pain in my leg was from the sciatic nerve. It hurt when I sat; it hurt when I lay down. Sometimes it hurt when I stood. Pain medication would not touch it. I learned how to exist with this new pain; I adjusted my life to the pain. I went to the chiropractor for treatments. It would leave for a little while, only to return in its fury once more. I went to the doctor and got an MRI; the results of the test were that I had a cyst in my spine and degenerative narrowing of the spine, and then he wanted to remove the cyst. I refused to have the surgery because of it being in the spinal column. I learned to live with it and compensated. The neck pain and the lower back pain still give me trouble today along with the muscles.

In 2008, I had a car wreck and broke my ankle. I had a temporary cast and it was fine for four days, then I went to the doctor for a new cast; that is when the pain started. My foot was swelling inside the cast, and in three days, I had the cast cut off. My foot was fiery red and swollen twice its size. I had RSD, Reactive Sympatric Dystrophy. My foot thought it was injured. I can honestly say this was the most pain I ever had. This pain was sharp like being stabbed. I went through different kinds of therapy, and I now walk with a cane. I still suffer with pain in my foot and ankle at times, especially on rainy days.

Now I shop with a scooter when the stores are large. Sometimes I take the walker with a seat so I can sit in stores when I get tired or my back hurts. I travel with the back brace, ankle bandages, and the knee brace just in case something goes out. I walk with a cane most of the time. Someone once said to me, "Physical suffering speeds up spiritual maturity. It really helps get our priorities right." It certainly did in my case. When physical suffering takes over one's life, there are two ways to go. You can get depressed because your health has been stolen from you and spend all your days in self-pity. Or, you can turn your life over to God, who created you in the beginning. That is what I chose to do.

The first thing I did when suffering came my way was pray. I asked for God to be with me and help me. I wanted Him to take away the pain or help me get through the pain, day-by-day. Sometimes people feel if God loves us, He will remove the agony. We forget He did not remove the thorn from Paul or the cross from Jesus.

As suffering continues, we should turn to the word and seek God's guidance. Everyone needs to hear God's word, so we can continue through the fiery furnace. God's word is full of the answers for our lives, even lives overwhelmed with anguish and woe, the bible always has the answers we need.

Cast all your anxiety on him because He cares about you.
1 Peter 5:7

Those words were very comforting to me in my world of pain. No one really knew the torture I was going through, except God. He told me He really cared about me. Everyone wants someone to care about him or her, especially when we are suffering.

Sometimes we let Satan steal our joy. He wants to distract us from looking to Jesus for our strength. We should be faithful to God in all circumstances. We should never give in, even in times of trouble. I know that we sometimes want to just give up. But we should stand strong in the Lord, be faithful to God, and keep our eyes on Jesus.

God always shows us a way out. He speaks to this in 1 Corinthians 10:13 about victory.

> No temptation has seized you accept what is common to man. And God is faithful; he will not let you be tempted beyond what you can bear. But when you are tempted, He will also provide a way out so that you can stand up under it.
>
> 1 Corinthians 10:13

I was tempted to give up and quit. There were times when I was ready to just lie in bed forever, or as long as it took to get well. But God, in His grace and mercy, showed me a way out though His word.

> And the God of all grace, who called you to his eternal glory in Christ, after you suffer for a little while, will himself restore you and make you strong, firm and steadfast.
>
> Peter 5:10

The promises of God are something we can cling to forever. God said I would suffer for only a little while. My time is God's time, so I must wait. God will release me from the suffering when it is time. I must trust God.

It is like the exercise of falling backwards into someone's arms and trusting they will catch you. Just to know God will make me strong, firm, and steadfast, I can get through the suffering in my life. Just to know God will support me, I can get through anything that comes my way.

When there is pain and turmoil in people's lives, they wait till they have no other place to go and then call on God. He is their last thought, their last chance to fix it. Why is that the way we act, putting God last when in our despair, He tells us that we should trust the Lord our God above all things? Yet, when people really need a friend, He's the last friend they call. Now, I know God can help in times of need. People, friends, or relatives cannot help me. I am a stranger here, and God alone is my refuge.

In my life, people have never solved a problem, stopped my tears, or brought me peace. They can't give me the comfort I really need or help make my choices. I know trusting God to comfort me and give me peace is God's plan for me. People are weak, like me, with human thoughts, like the world. God has us on His mind all the time. We should always turn to Him first; that is the right choice.

Some people would say my life of pain was a sad life. I would tell them my life in the presence of God and His mercy is a blessed life. I can only praise Him for making me one of His children. To be used by Him, humbles me. God said He would use the weak to shame the proud, and I am truly the weak. God lifts me up daily, and He uses me to tell other people about the Lord and Savior Jesus Christ. He uses me to encourage other people to be the best they can be for Jesus. He uses me to give hope to the hopeless.

You may think that I had bad health in my life, and I did, physically, but my spiritual health was very good. I was going to live forever because of Jesus. I was at peace and not in turmoil; I was content with my life. I was very happy, and there was lots of joy inside of me. The measure of love God gave me outweighed the bad times. My life has been a journey through pain, but I can tell you, I would not change it at all. I learned to love my life because of the blessing God gave me.

I wanted to be like other people; I just wanted to be normal. I was unable to do simple tasks like other wives and mothers. I looked like others, but I certainly did not act like them. One day many years ago the telephone rang about a job interview. They wanted me to be a teller at a local bank. The pay was good, the hours great, and it seemed perfect for a normal person. I had prayed to get a job. I wanted to go to work when the boys were gone from home and be busy. But my illness was so bad that somewhere deep down inside, I knew I would have trouble just holding this perfect job, so I refused it. I felt like I had no purpose in this world. It seemed like my only purpose was to suffer with muscular dystrophy.

I felt like a discarded person, spending many hours each week waiting for someone to need me when the boys were gone to school. I prayed I would not be ill anymore, and the pain would leave. I needed to trust God with my life. I needed to surrender my will to the will of God, and He would show me the way to live. The Bible says to

> Trust in the Lord with all your heart and lean not on your own understanding; in all your ways acknowledge Him, and He will make your paths straight.
>
> Proverbs 3:5–6

That is what I needed to do. I couldn't go on trying to be like others when God directed me to live for Him. God has all the answers: He alone heals. The Bible says,

> Who forgives all your sins and heals all your diseases, who redeems your life from the pit and crowns you with love and compassion.
>
> Psalm 103:3–4

He could redeem me from the pit I was in.

I needed to trust God with my life. My illness may not leave, but God was always with me. Year after year I prayed for healing. Then one day when I was praying, I gave up praying to be like others, and a peace came over me. I learned to live in God's presence, and living for Him became my purpose. He is my healer, my redeemer, and my savior. God has been with me through this pain-filled life. He alone is there to comfort me, and He turns my tears to joy. He walks with me daily, holding me in His arms, and loves me more than I deserve. God lifts me up when I am down; He is where my strength comes from. When I look to Him, I am not weak and in pain, I am strong.

I know God's grace and His mercy for me. His suffering on the cross was more intense than any I endured. He died on the cross for me because of my sin. He hung there gasping for air. Beaten without mercy, the blood from His wounds dripped down to the ground. He did it all so I could live without fear of death. He did it for all mankind, and His love for me is the greatest love there is.

God took away all my fear, the fear I had of the future with muscular dystrophy; the fear I had of my present life in pain. God has given me hope, joy, peace, and love. I still live with pain, but He is the reason I can live a life that reflects a whole person; I reflect Jesus.

2 PETER 3:16

"This is what he says in all his letters when he writes on the subject. There are some difficult things in his letters, which ignorant and unstable people explain falsely, as they do with other passages of the Scriptures. So they bring on their own destruction."

Paul was writing to us. He was warning us to beware of people who are ignorant about the word of God. Not all people can understand the word of God because it was God inspired and only the Holy Spirit can help people to understand the truth of God's word.

People would like the word of God to fit into their way of thinking. But man's mind is too small. The Bible instructs us to pray and ask God for wisdom before we read, then rely on the Holy Spirit to make it clear to us. And accept God's word as a small child.

MY HEART BELONGS TO YOU

We are all God's children and when we know this, we are strong. My heart seems to be the tender part of my body. It's easily broken, and people can hurt it. My mind is strong but confused at times, it keeps my heart from peace.

If I use my mind to reason and make choices on my own, I get into trouble. I heard the saying, "We have freedom of choice." Without God's control, we seem to make choices that are selfish and bad for us. If I fix my eyes on Jesus and let God have control over my life, things go better for me. If my life is in the control of God, it flows like a beautiful river. My heart belongs to Jesus.

Today is another day of total pain. The pain is surging through every part of my body, my back, chest, neck, and limbs. I need my Savior to be my refuge today. I give my tender heart to Jesus to keep safe. I need a Savior to help me deal with the world of pain and agony in which I live.

I need the Lord to empower me, to overcome. I pray my mind be filled with thoughts of my Lord and not of pain. Today, I need the love only God has for me. God is my strength to carry on in a world filled with imperfection. Jesus gave me a reason to live a life of peace and joy because I am His and my heart belongs to Him. I was lost, but now I am found, and the pain means nothing because I am saved and I will live without pain one day.

I Want to Be Like Them

I want to be like them, I just want to be normal. Not different, but normal, like those other people. I am different, very different, because I am unable to do what everyone else can do. I look normal! But I am not.

I guess you have noticed, I am pretty frustrated today. It all started Monday when I went for another job interview. They called me from a resume I had mailed to them months before. I went to this interview for the perfect job. It was a bank teller position; the hours were nine to two. The pay was right, hours good, just a perfect job for me.

I have prayed for six months that I would get a job to replace the one I lost. God provided everyone around me with work when they needed a job, now I prayed it was my turn. I also prayed that if I got this job that God would also make me capable to do it.

Somehow when this phone call came I wanted to believe I was going to get well and be like everyone else. I wanted to get up and have a reason to be up. This would be the answer to my prayer, but four days have passed and no call back from the bank. I have no one home during the day, my children are grown and on their own. My husband works two jobs and is gone from home over seventy hours a week. I wished I'd have some purpose in this life from day-to-day. I struggled all week with why I was left here to sit alone and not be useful anymore.

I know of people who live alone, and they are discarded people who feel this way. I spent a lot of time lying in bed waiting for someone to need me. I prayed God would heal me from this illness, but it will be God's will if I were healed.

I don't do much around my house because of my illness I hire it all done. People come in and do my house cleaning and gardening. I even have a handy man to help with odd jobs. I live like a princess, so it seems. I only want to be useful; everyone wants to be useful in this world. I was not satisfied with my life this week wanting to be something I am not. Where does my help come from? My help comes from the Lord. I am sad and tired of being different.

I turned on Christian TV and it was 1:00 a.m. when I was writing this and unable to sleep. The lady was speaking about God's Word she said to turn to Psalm 103:3–4, so I did and it said,

> Who forgives all your sins and heals all your diseases, who redeems your life from the pit and crowns you with love and compassion.
>
> Psalm 103:3–4

My eyes were on self-pity. Poor me I'm different, I'm ill, and I can't do what others can. God almighty will redeem me from this pit. If I get this job, I must know it is because God wants me to have it because it is part of His plan for my life. If I do not get this job, it will be because this was not Gods plan for me. He has made other plans, and I will be content, and there will be no fear and no sorrow.

I throw myself into these depressed states when I wonder why my life is the way it is, and why I'm not like others. When I turn to God and keep focus on Jesus, I know why I'm here. I am just a child of God and my purpose is to do His will. God needs me to carry on His work, and He wants to guide me all the way. He doesn't want His child to be sad because He loves me so much. I am very important to my Lord. Jesus even died for me so I could live for Him.

No one loves me more than this. God promises me in heaven there will be no pain, no sorrow, no tears, and He has prepared a place for me. Jesus is my Lord and my Savior. I have all I need here on earth while I wait to go back home.

Tripped Up

I am not confused about what I want to do. I want to live my life for Jesus Christ. Not because I have to, but because it is what my heart leads me to do. I can think of nothing in this world that can satisfy my heart's longing.

Tonight, on my way to the advent service at church, I delivered my last Avon order for Christmas. In the dark of the night, I tripped up some stairs. Oh, I didn't fall, and I thanked God. To some, this would be just a minor trip up, but not for me, my time was limited. Things seemed okay, but about forty-five minutes later it happened: pain all over, not just simple aches and pains, but real pain. It hit with a vengeance, and I was helpless to its cruel attack. It is now one o'clock in the morning and I cannot sleep for the pain medicine has worn off, and I'm left alone again to write my thoughts. I had thoughts of God, thoughts of God's purpose for my life, and thoughts of the Savior. These thoughts ease the pain that travels to every limb. What could God possibly want with me?

He says He wants each of us. In my life God has filled my heart with Himself, and I am just a Christian who believes what God has promised. Tonight I went to church, and I couldn't even stand up. Tears streamed down my cheeks, tears of pain. I was determined not to leave the service. I prayed for God almighty to fill my heart with words of renewal. This is what God can do for each one of us if we just listen to Him.

Tonight, I heard we needed nothing from this earth; we need no reward or praise because we live by God's grace alone. I gained strength when I knew I was here only to live for Christ. The pastor said we should not give up or let up, we should live for the cause of Christ. My hope is in Christ the Bible says,

Remember the word to your servant, for you have given me hope. My comfort in my suffering is this: Your promise preserves my life.

Psalms 119:49–50

This is exactly how I feel. Through Jesus' death for me, I am made new; He has left me the Holy Spirit and His word.

I tripped up some stairs tonight, but I didn't get tripped up. I got built up and renewed. Pain is a funny thing, when it hits me I go right to God for help. God's promises to me are found everywhere. I look in the Bible,

> And the God of all grace, who called you to His eternal glory in Christ, after you have suffered a little while, will himself restore you and make you strong, firm and steadfast. To him is the power forever and ever.
>
> 1 Peter 5:10–11

Tonight I tripped up some steps, but I thank God for everything in my life. He helps me to see very clearly throughout my life lessons. I may be weak at times in body, but in heart, I am strong through the Holy Spirit's guidance. God said,

> Your sun will never set again, and your moon will wane no more; the Lord will be your everlasting light, and you days of sorrow will end.
>
> Isaiah 60:20

Praise God for allowing me to trip up and for helping me when I fall down.

His Divine Power

> If you remain in me and my words abide in you, ask what you wish, and it will be given you.
>
> John 15:7

This was the verse I heard Monday morning at 8:15 a.m. on my way to prayer group at church. It really was exactly the verse I needed this day. And God knew it. Let me back up and tell you why I needed this verse.

Sunday night I was very angry and nervous, and I didn't know why. The only explanation could be PMS. My husband Gib asked just what was wrong with me, and my reply was, "Don't talk to me; just hug me." So he did. I thought it would have left by morning, but no, I was still in the same state. I tried to talk to my husband, but inside I wanted to argue, I wanted to be right. I just couldn't shake these feelings. I ask Gib to let me be right just today, and he could be right the rest of the month. I just wanted to avoid an argument. He gave me a kiss and hurried off to work. I didn't blame him, I wanted to get away from myself too! I was very cranky.

I said my prayers at home and asked God to show me a way to get through this day. I asked that this angry, sinful person be forgiven. I certainly didn't want to be this way I wasn't myself. Oh, maybe my old self, but not the child of God I usually am now that Jesus came into my life. Today I was like the little girl with that curl in the middle of my forehead: "when she was good, she was very good, and when she was bad, she was horrid."

I pulled into the church parking lot and prayed, asking and expecting God almighty to answer. I asked for God to guide my day and to lead me in the way I should go and to take all this sinful feeling from me. I asked Him to set me free. I asked to be filled with the Holy Spirit to rule and reign in my life, I wanted to be used by God, and I wanted to abide in Him.

I couldn't believe the change of heart that came over me. I was made new and had no anger, no nervousness, and no PMS. I was saved once again from this world and my own sinful self. The rest of my day was full of turmoil, confusion, and "sheer joy." How could this be the rest of my day? Well, no matter what, confusion was in my midst or how much turmoil was presented to me, I had inexpressible and glorious joy inside me.

Come Near to God

Every day I live here on earth, the Lord, my Lord, shows His presence to me. I know He is with me always. Some may say today was a sad day. I say every day with the Lord Jesus in my life is a great day.

Rose, a lady from our church, went to live with Jesus today. She knew and loved her Savior Jesus Christ. She knew Jesus died and rose just for her, so she would live eternally with Him, and that is where she is now. Rose found her strength through Christ and persevered throughout this year. She was in very poor health for years. But this year, she really suffered as she watched her husband and son-in-law go home to God before her. Now Rose has joined her loved ones in a place Christ prepared just for her.

Over eighty years ago, Rose was born a preacher's daughter. I figure she must have always known and loved Jesus. She knew the love that only comes from God.

This evening on my way to Bible study, I made a stop at a friend's house and she told me some disturbing news. She told me Paul, Gib's cousin's husband, who suffered and endured so much this year, had yet another trial. This past February, just eight short months ago, Paul had a stroke on the first day of his retirement. Brain surgery was required and a long recovery, as his right arm and leg were affected, thus causing him to go to therapy and exercising every day.

This summer he was in swimming exercise class that I led. He worked so hard to recover the use of his arm and leg. Faithfully, twice a week, he and others exercised to restore the use of arms and legs. Paul's eyes would twinkle, as I would tell him to join hands with his wife Betty and do side steps as the music played. They danced once again in the water.

My friend told me Paul was in the hospital. She said the doctors opened him up to solve a problem and there was only sadness all over his body, cancer. Just a short time left before he will be home with the Lord. I guess Paul and his wife Betty will have to have their next dance in heaven. But this is not a sad time, because God has written his promises to us in his book the Bible. In the book of James, God says,

> Come near to God and He will come near to you.
>
> James 4:8

Paul and Rose came near to God this past year, and God was with them. God comforted them and strengthened them. God brought peace to them and their families. I am praying for Paul, lifting him up to the Lord Jesus, so he may have that peace that passes all understanding. In Isaiah 26:3, God said,

> You will keep in perfect peace him whose mind is steadfast, because he trusts in you.
>
> Isaiah 26:3

We need to seek the promises of God that He reveals through his word.

Tonight in my Bible study, I was sad thinking of the tears my friends must have. So I excused myself and called Betty, Paul's wife. I told her of my love for her and Paul, and I assured her of Jesus' love for both of them. "Our strength comes from our Lord and from nowhere else," I said. Tonight the Bible study was full of grace and peace; we spoke of our significance in Christ. He is all we need in every situation.

I lift my eyes to the hills, where does my help come from? My help comes from the Lord the maker of heaven and earth.

Psalms 121:1–2

So this was a good day because this was a day that the Lord did make, so let us all rejoice. We should rejoice for everything, we should rejoice in our suffering because through our suffering we "come near to God." That is all we think of when our time on earth grows short, coming nearer to God so He can come nearer to us. We want His presence, for in His presence there is comfort. I pray that whoever reads this, will remember God's promise in Romans,

May the God of hope fill you with all joy and peace, as you trust in Him, so that you may overflow with hope by the power of the Holy Spirit.

Romans 15:13

When we know Jesus as our Savior we will live forever.

Prayer

The word is near you; it is in your mouth and in your heart.

Romans 10:8

Today is Wednesday, and His word was near me today. I felt His presence near me all day long. In my prayers today I said, "Use this humble servant," and praised God, He uses me, and I thank Him.

This was like any other Wednesday. I awoke and began to pray, thanking God for yesterday, and thanking Him for this very day. I prayed for forgiveness and cleansing, and I prayed for God to be with my family all day. I thanked Him for all my loved ones, and then prayed for others. At the end of my prayers, I always asked God to equip me and use me.

Today I was going to a Bible study in the park, so I prayed for God to bring those whom He wanted to the park. For the last two weeks I had only one attend the study, but I thanked God for that one He sent to learn Hs word. I know God is in charge so we did the study with only the two of us. But today was different; He sent us one more now there are three.

The study began, Nell and Anne were eager to study Gods word. This was Nell's first time, and I noticed there was a sharp wind. At first it wasn't too bad, but the longer we sat, the colder we became. We were going to hear God's word today, and nothing would stop the will of God.

We talked about how the Bible is full of spiritual blessing we can claim as believers. We talked about the three resources we have to live a Christian life. We have the Holy Spirit, the Bible, and Prayer. We searched the scriptures and found that when the Spirit comes to live in us, we have new life and every believer has the indwelling Spirit. We talked about the Bible and how it tells us what God wants us to do. We learned the Bible is the life-giving breath of God; it is God's communication with man. He wants us to read it, obey it, and believe it.

Everything to this point was normal. But God had a plan for us we didn't even know about. We began talking about prayer, where and when we should pray. We learned how to pray and whom we should pray for and that all the answers were in the Bible. When we came to 1 John 5:14–15, which says,

> This is the confidence we have in approaching God; that if we ask anything according to His will, He hears us. And if we know that He hears us, whatever we ask, we know that we have what we asked of Him.
>
> John 5:14–15

This is when Nell's eyes filled with tears. I kept talking, assuring her that we may not understand now why things happen, but it is God's will and all things bring us closer to Christ. She was weeping now, I didn't know why. Her tears were streaming down her face and hitting the tabletop. By this time the wind was so strong and so cold we were getting uncomfortable.

I had been praying silently for the weather not to chase us off and for God to free us from this torment. I couldn't understand why the wind was so strong now. Then Nell stood up excused herself and began to walk down into the valley of the park. I asked Anne to pray with me for Nell. Not knowing what upset her, I prayed for God to comfort her and bring her back and whatever her sadness was that God restore her. When the prayer was over Anne, was crying because of her compassion and love.

When Nell returned, Anne shared her coat with her and I passed out tissues. Then Nell spoke. She said she had not prayed for two years because her mother and father had both died of cancer and she had prayed for them, but they still suffered. She couldn't understand why godly people had to suffer. The scripture spoke to her heart. She always loved God but just couldn't pray anymore. It was like the dike had broken and all the pent up prayers of Nell's heart were released that day.

She spoke of how her mother longed to be with Jesus, and how much she loved her mother. Her son was born, and he had some kind of trouble. The doctors told her he would never walk. Then her father got sick. She prayed and prayed for healing, but her father went to heaven too. Nell was lost and alone; her communication with God had stopped. Oh, she went to church, praised God, and sang to him, but she just couldn't pray to God because of her parents. Her son did walk and was just fine, but she still couldn't pray.

At the end of class, we were all to say one thanksgiving sentence of prayer. I thanked God for freedom to study His word. Anne thanked God for helping her husband during his stroke. Then Nell said, "Thank you Lord for healing my son." God restored her prayer life. Prayer is our communication with God; Nell was free from her pain and was closer to God. Nell is God's child, and His will for us is always good. Our lives are to glorify God.

After the study was over, the sun came out and the wind died down. I guess Satan was upset because he could see Nell was being restored today. All the bitter cold wind couldn't stop the will of God. Satan lost once again. He is the loser, and God is always victorious! The temperature was fifty degrees at 10:30 a.m. It was too cold for July 5. Nell's tears washed away the sadness, and Gods love restored her through prayer.

What If

Today is the seventh day of November, what if December 31 was the last day of our lives and January 1 was the Day of the Lord? You know, the day when Jesus returns to come as King of Kings and Lord of Lords, when Jesus comes to kill and destroy the evil forces of wickedness? Are you ready for the Day of the Lord?

What if He really came then? What if there were only fifty-eight days till that great day, are you ready? How would you act, what would you do? What if it were true? The Bible tells of His coming again in glory. What if it were really, really true and in eight weeks and two days we would see Jesus. What if?

I believe we should all live as if Jesus were coming today. We should all be ready to be called in a moment. Some may question what to do and how to live your life with a "what if" attitude. Well, I live as if it were my last day on earth every day.

Every morning I wake up and pray to my God. I pray for guidance and forgiveness. I give up prayers of thankfulness to my God. I intercede for others and lift them up to Him. I pray, "Use me Lord to do your will. Empty me and fill me with your Holy Spirit." Then I arise with a thankful heart, knowing God has a purpose for me.

When I go outside, I realize that God is everywhere. I see his beauty in His trees and His flowers. I see Jesus when I look up, and there are beautiful clouds. I thank God every time I see a beautiful bird in my yard. I know God loves me and will provide for me like he provides for those birds. I truly am willing to surrender my plans to His plans. This is a day the Lord has made, let me rejoice and live in it.

With this morning attitude, the day is truly blessed, and God will call on me to tell people about the love Jesus has for them. I will keep a positive attitude, and sadness will not be around me because I have a Savior. This day I spoke about Jesus to two Christian friends in affirmation to lift them up. Then I went to another friends for coffee and nine women read God's Word. Colossians 3:17 said,

> And whatever you do, whether in the word or in deed, do it in the name of the Lord Jesus, giving thanks to God the Father through Him.
>
> Colossians 3:17

That is truly the attitude we should possess at all times. If we allow the Holy Spirit who indwells in us to have control over us, we could obey these words.

After lunch, I read God's Word and did some work from a Bible study I'm in. God is so good, and I'm proud to be His child. Then I gave some food away to the boy scouts. I drove home to rest and prayed all the way home; prayers of praise and tears filled my eyes as I once more told Jesus how much I loved Him. The words coming from the radio said, "Jesus was my only hope." When I got home, I rested.

When I awoke I picked up my precious grandchild from daycare, and as we drove home we sang "Jesus Loves Me" and her little eyes lit up. I praised God for her. We played till supper, and her mom came for her. I ate supper with my husband. Then the phone rang. "Hello, are you the lady who does the jail ministry?"

"Yes," I replied.

"I want you to pray for me," she sobbed. We talked about fifteen minutes. Her name was Mary, and she was crying because she was alone. She had no family or friends where she was in Florida, and she was very upset.

I told her Jesus was with her, and He knew exactly why she was sad. His promise to us is to never leave us nor forsake us, and He would be with her forever. I asked Mary if she felt a big empty place in her heart and she replied yes. I said, "Sometimes we try to fill that empty place with friends, husbands, lovers, or children. Some even try drugs or alcohol, but no matter what you do to fill the empty spot, it is still empty because this place is a special place God made for Jesus' spirit to live in you. If you would allow Him to fill that place, the darkness and emptiness would be filled with the light and love of Jesus." I prayed over the telephone with Mary, I never knew her last name, but God does.

As soon as I hung up the phone, I left for jail to do a Bible study with three inmates. We talked about how all people are sinners, and the more we know about sin, the more we realize just what Jesus did when He saved us. We talked about how our lives are to bring glory to God, and that He has a purpose for each one of us.

One girl is charged with accessory to murder; she is nineteen years old and has been in jail one year already with me. God has a purpose for her too. She was a heavy drug user for years, and now she reads God's word every day and wants to serve Him. She came from a very abusive family, and God saved her life, so He could bless her with His grace. I praised God all the way home in the car that night. He is truly an almighty God to change hearts and minds of girls who ran from Him.

When I got home, I called my mother and talked to my husband. I then went to bed and prayed to God, thanking Him for using me and loving me and saving me this day. Now it is 1:00 a.m. and there are fifty-seven days till December 31st. What if this was the last year of your life? Are you allowing God to use you to bring glory to Him? Are you fulfilling your purpose He has already planned for you on the way you should go? What if you only have fifty-seven days left? How would you live your life?

White Horse

I saw heaven standing open and there before me was a white horse whose rider is called faithful and true.

Revelations 19:11

I never really thought much about Jesus coming again in glory. I was so thrilled and excited by Christmas and the Savior of the whole world coming as a baby, a baby so innocent coming just to die. How awesome God is to capture this moment in a manger filled with straw. No grandeur, just simple straw and lowly animals.

Christmas, for a long time, was my favorite time of the year, with beautiful music about the Christ child and snow and beauty everywhere. This is God's plan, with shepherds and wise men, camels and donkeys. A perfect time to rejoice; the Savior is born. I learned more about God and spent more time in prayer and studied His word. More and more years passed with children of my own growing big and strong. I always tried to show them the true beauty of Christmas, to let them know the Christ Child I learned to love so much.

As my own children grew and my love for to developed more and more each day, I began to think about why Jesus came to this earth. Tears swelled up in my eyes when I thought, *He came to save all people.* To die for you and me, He was no longer a baby but a Savior and Redeemer. As I meditated more on his death and resurrection, I began to love Him even more. The Lord my God has given me wisdom I could not have gotten on my own. I am learning to trust Him more and see His blessings all around.

Then one day it became perfectly clear to me. I loved my sons so much by now, I would die for them, but to give one of them up to death, no! I couldn't, this would just be too painful. *Dear God, you gave up your Son for me.* I thought, *I am not worthy; I don't deserve this kind of love. Oh! How much you really love me.*

This death on the cross is because of me; I helped drive those nails one-by-one because of my sins. Now with Easter approaching, I attend all the Lenten services; I need those weeks to prepare my heart for His ultimate sacrifice.

I couldn't tell you which time of the year means the most to me now: His coming to earth as a baby or His leaving this earth as my Redeemer. God assures me of my eternal life with Him, I am overjoyed and overflowing with the great news of my Savior's love for me.

God allowed me to grow in knowledge. I learned to pray continually and learned God does answer prayers. I began studying God's word, longing to know Him more. I longed to praise my Lord in song. I know the Holy Spirit's presence was now in my life, and I turned my life over completely to God. I learned I was a shell of a person without Jesus living through me. Christ in me, and I in Him. This child of God is growing in Christ. My love for the Lord is increasing. I began leading Bible studies only through Christ's empowerment, and I let the Holy Spirit lead me. By the grace of God I am receiving many blessings. Peace and joy surround me. My life is not important, but the life I live for the Lord is truly a blessing. I trust in the Lord with the assurance that He will never leave me. I can do all things in Christ who strengthens me.

Then one day, a free cassette tape arrived in the mail. It spoke of the Lamb of God who would return one day for us. The clouds in the sky were billowy that day, as white as the horse carrying the king. All of a sudden tears were streaming down my face. God knew I was ready for more of His wisdom and knowledge.

The God of Majesty and faithfulness would rule and reign with victory. I realized His eyes would be like fire and His head fully crowned. The Lamb would ride in judgment. The tears were really flowing. Jesus will return not with a crown of thorns, and there will be no cross of pain. He will come in Glory to take His throne. He will come as King of Kings and Lord of Lords.

This knowledge gives me the hope I lacked. Shortly after that day, what looked like junk mail was in the mailbox. I looked through all of it, and there among the coupons and sweepstakes entries was His picture. Just a poster, but there He was in all His glory upon a white horse, my King of Kings and Lord of Lords. A red cape blew as he rode. His head was covered with a full crown. His face was sure of victory. He was in those same white clouds I saw that day, and all around Him was His name. The poster said Prince of Peace, Morning Star, Redeemer, Alpha and Omega, Emanuel, Jesus, Lord, King of Kings, Lamb of God, Messiah, Good Shepherd, Christ, and Son of God.

The expectation I have now is one of complete excitement. I know there is a Savior who redeemed me, and now I have eternal life. This Savior is my Lord, and He gave me the peace and joy in my life. Now I know Christ will return on a white horse, this is my hope.

God is not finished with me yet. There is a lot to learn, and God is my teacher. I am His, and He will fill me to over flow with his rich blessings. Knowing He will return for his people, I will bless His name with a thankful heart. Behold the lamb will come upon a white horse and when He returns we all will hail with one accord the King of Kings and Lord of Lords.

GALATIANS 3:16

"The promises were spoken to Abraham and to his seed. The scriptures does not say 'and to seeds,' meaning many people, but 'and to your seed,' meaning one person who is Christ."

Jesus Christ the Messiah was promised to us way back in Abraham's day and before. Jesus would come to save His people and He would come through Abraham's line. This was a promise to Abraham. We too are promised many things from God. The greatest promise is that the blood of the Lamb, Jesus, forgives our sins. The second greatest promise is that Jesus will return to claim His people.

Abraham's promise came true just as God said. His blood was shed on Calvary for the forgiveness of sin. This promise comes true for all who know Jesus and are washed in the waters of baptism.

It is also promised that Jesus will return on the last day. This is going to be fulfilled and He will come for us. As we say, "Come Lord Jesus, come, today."

MOM, MY BEST FRIEND

My mom became my best friend, as I grew older. We spent lots of time together over the years. We joined garden club, extension club, and later Red Hatters. We went to ceramics, painting, aerobics, and the spa. We played bridge, took cooking classes, shopped, and just had fun together. We had lunch together three times a week.

She was there with the raising of the boys. We would sit by her pool for hours on a hot summer afternoon just talking about everything. We shared our dreams and secrets. We would cook together when there were big crowds of people at her place; we would fix food for the multitudes. And my best friend would always be there on holidays, and we would share more than being best friends; we would share a mother- daughter relationship, too.

I talked to my mom every day for hours and hours. It is hard to write this part of my book, because my best friend in the entire world is with Jesus now. But I always want to remember the fun we had. I miss my mom, but I think I miss my best friend more. She was always there for me when I was sad or confused; she always listened when I wanted to complain. I could share my thoughts with her when no one else cared. I always had someone to do things with and was never alone; she was just a phone call away. Most girls only dream of this kind of relationship with their moms, and I had one.

Mom and I bought new tennis outfits one year so we could play tennis in the park. Then my parents built a tennis court so we could play every day. We looked so good in our new outfits. We went to the spa and exercised; this called for a new outfit. Then there was the aerobic class, one more new outfit. We volunteered at the hospital together, and they gave us matching jackets. I guess the Red Hat Club was the best, because we also got to wear hats with our new outfits.

In some of the clubs, there was no call for an outfit. In garden club, we entered flower shows. This was a place where we got to wear the clothes we bought when we shopped. We called ourselves *professional consumers*. We were able to consume at any given moment; we were on call to the mall. What fun we had laughing and being together.

Once we went away on a bus tour to the Wisconsin Dells. We spent many hours on the bus just laughing. We sat in the back of the bus because we were the *rowdies*. If you wanted to have fun, you just hung around us. At ceramics we laughed so much Betty, one of the gals who went there, called it her therapy session.

When we volunteered at the hospital, we would work at the snack bar and decorate the display windows in the hallways. We drove hospital meals on wheels to the shut-ins. When times were tough, we were together. When times were great, we were together. I also had a regular relationship with her just as mother and daughter. We would go on family vacations and do family things together. Like other families, we had our birthdays and holidays. When I was sick, my mom would come take care of me. When I would get behind in my work, my mom would come and fold my laundry. She would baby-sit for the boys when I needed her. I really loved being with my mom at all times, and I wanted her to be involved in my life.

Before my mom went to heaven, she was blind. We spent a lot of time together. She was always with me just to get out of the house. I sold Avon, and she would ride with me to make deliveries. I would throw the rolled up books out the window onto the driveways. When mom would help I would drive up to the driveway and say throw. She would blindly throw the book out the window then say, "Did I make it?" And then we would laugh.

Anyone who knew us recognized the special relationship we had, loving to be together. I never regretted anything, I spent the time I needed with my mom, and I had forty years of friendship and sixty years being her daughter. No one could ever replace my mom, and when she left, I just thanked God I had a mom for sixty years. Some girls have their moms for shorter times. I never tried to replace my mom, but I did try to replace the friendship I had with her, and that was the hardest for me; I needed a friend.

I was sad and lonely after she left. I wanted to talk to someone on the phone, I wanted to shop with someone, and I wanted someone to go to the spa with me. Now I found my self shopping alone and eating lunch alone. There was a big dark hole in my heart where my Mom lived. I prayed for God to send me someone who would be my friend.

God is good. He started to replace my mom's friendship with others. It took Mary, Martha, and Mo, just to replace Mom. Mary hears my secret thoughts; she will listen to me talk about my love for Jesus. She is my soul mate. She keeps me from being sad by pointing me to Jesus. I thank God for Mary.

Martha fills the gap. She is the one who I play games with and shop with. She goes to the spa with me. She is a Red Hatter, and we go to lunch. She cares for me when I am ill. Martha is faithful. I thank God for putting Martha into my life.

Then God gave me Mo; that is short for Molesia. She is the one God sent to talk to me on the phone for hours. We go to lunch or she will bring me breakfast. When I'm with her, it's as if I was a young girl with my girlfriends once more. We share our dreams and hopes for the future. She is generous and loving. I am glad she is my friend.

It took three to replace the friend I had in my mom. But, God is faithful. He knew what I needed and sent them to me: Mary, Martha, and Mo. We all need someone to keep us hopeful and looking to the future. That's what friends are for; they go through the good times and the bad with us. They are there to lean on when we need propping up. I could not have made it through this short life without the good friends God sent. There is only a bridge over the hole in my heart, because there are days I long for my Mom.

I always try to be the best friend I can to everyone I call friend. I listen to them and try to be there for them when they are sad. I encourage them and try to give them hope. I tell all of them about Jesus who died for them. That's what friends do. We all need a friend and we all need to be one.

I was a friend to my boys as they grew up, and we are still friends today. I have a mother-son relationship too. I know I have a place in the heart of my sons, and that place will only be filled with me. No one will ever be able to replace me like no one can replace my mom. Maybe they can replace the friendship I had with her, but no one can replace a mom.

MATTHEW 3:16

"And Jesus, when he was baptized, went up straightway out of the water; and lo, the heavens were opened unto him, and he saw the Spirit of God descending like a dove, and lighting upon him."

When we are baptized in the waters of baptism, the Holy Spirit of God descends upon us and we are made new. The Holy Spirit of God dwells in us and we have the power of God. We can now have the strength to overcome things that bind us to our old life of sin.

All we need to do is trust in the Lord and the power we now have, following and obeying His word, and not fall back into our old life. We should live with the hope of heaven in our sights, knowing our future is with God in heaven. For the heavens are open to us for an eternity.

DEATH IS BEAUTIFUL

Before I was a Christian, I was afraid of death. I really wasn't around anyone who died and did not understand why it happened. When I had my first brush with death, I was eleven years old. It was a very warm summer night and very muggy. We were sitting on our breezeway and waved at the neighbors who were sitting on their front porch, eating cantaloupe with a scoop of ice cream in it. They went inside and in a few minutes, the ambulance arrived and hauled the lady out; she was dead. I wondered if it was the cantaloupe or the ice cream that did it. I didn't know, but I was never going to put those two together.

When I was in the ninth grade, I sang in the choir at school. We were performing at a Lutheran school for the men's club banquet. We were about done with our performance of *Swing Low Sweet Chariot*. I was standing front row, center. Our director was a vigorous man and was swinging his arm to direct us. We were on the last stanza were it says, *Coming for to carry me home*, when the choir director dropped dead at my feet. He was dead instantly. I'd never been to a funeral, and they asked me to sing the songs he wrote with a quartet at his funeral and I said, "No." I didn't know how I could even speak at a funeral, much less sing.

I still did not understand death and was afraid to get too close to it. My grandmother died when I was about seventeen and I did not want to go to her funeral, so I volunteered to take care of my little brother David. I had still never been to a funeral or funeral home to see the dead people.

When I was eighteen, my boyfriend's grandpa died, and I thought it was safe to go to the funeral of a man I never met so I went. I was all right at first, and then I began to cry, no, wail uncontrollably. I cried louder than anyone there. I couldn't stop. What came over me? How could I cry so loudly for a stranger?

At twenty-five, I came to know Jesus as my Savior. I learned that death was just the beginning, not the end. I was given a gift of living forever with the Lord. I learned that heaven is the better place, and we should look forward to being there. What a relief!

The dead are not just dead, but they live forever with God in Heaven if they know Jesus. I was no longer afraid to go to funerals or be at funeral homes with the people who had left for heaven. Oh, to have the faith of a child. When my husband's mother died, my nine-year-old son Timmy went with us to the funeral home. He was in Lutheran school and he knew Jesus as his Savior. When the families were gathered for the first viewing and weeping because of their loss, my son went to each one and said, "Don't cry, Grandma is in heaven with Jesus." He understood death and was comforting others. He was not afraid of death. He knew what it was all about and he was nine.

Many years ago, I found I had a Savior, Jesus Christ, who did give up His life for me. But before He left this earth, He said He would leave us his Spirit to live in us all the days of our lives, if we believed. The Holy Spirit would comfort us and equip us for service. I learned to rely on His Spirit whenever I spoke of Jesus or His Word. I learned that when I pray, I pray through this Spirit and I am never without the Word of God and the power of God inside of me.

I was on the evangelism team at our church. Before we went out to call on people to tell them about Jesus, we would pray. The first time the pastor asked me to pray was a real test for me. I prayed silently all my life, even when I was not saved, but never out loud. I remember the words he said, "Pat, would you lead us in prayer this evening." I said, "Yes."

We all bowed our heads and closed our eyes, and I waited for the Lord to lead me. There was silence in the room, but I knew I had the Holy Spirit within me. I knew I would not have to pray on my own but that the Spirit would strengthen me. So I waited. I waited for God to bring the words to my mind that I needed that evening.

We were becoming uncomfortable with the silence. Then all of a sudden Margaret, an elderly lady, jumped out of her chair and scurried to the door to leave the room. I waited a few more seconds, and then the words came flowing out of me. I was calm and at peace because of the Spirit that was in me.

When the prayer was over and Margaret returned, she apologized for leaving the room. She had gone into the hallway to laugh. She said, "I never heard Pat with nothing to say." Everyone in the room laughed in agreement. I could pray out loud now that the big step was over. When Thanksgiving came that year, the aunts, uncles, and cousins were gathered; my mom asked me to pray before the meal. I did and prayed at every Thanksgiving while we were together. In the prayer, I thanked God for His Son Jesus who died and rose for us so we could be saved and asked for blessing on the food.

When my godfather died, he was the first to go home to heaven in our family since I first prayed years ago. The youngest of three brothers, for a long time my uncle was on my prayer list and now he was in heaven. As the evening ended, and only the family was left, we gathered around my uncle. Everyone was crying, but inside I was rejoicing, because my first grandchild was due at any moment. My uncle was going to enter heaven, and heaven was sending me my granddaughter, Jourdan.

There was no minister to pray that evening at the funeral home, and my cousins asked me to pray. We bowed our heads, there was no waiting, and the words of joy and comfort flowed through my lips. The Spirit of God was there to comfort my family. He was there to give them peace. I was at the funeral home praying out loud for others.

Jesus said he would leave us someone to speak for Him and that Spirit would live in us. I was calm and at peace when I prayed because of God's presence in my life. Now death was not frightening, and I could comfort others because I understood that life is eternal. I no longer wailed with big tears; I have an understanding about death.

My dad had two brushes with death before God called him home. In August of 2000, my family was going to Vacation Bible School. I had a full week of telling the little children about God's love for them. I starred in a play that started each night's activities. The children's eyes lit up when the actors would come on the stage and begin telling how God provides everything they need.

When the week of activities was over on Friday evening, my husband and I went out of town as soon as the last play was finished. We spent the next few days out of town with our children and grandchildren for one of our family vacations.

We were very tired when we returned. I felt like I was living in a whirlwind. I was home about forty-five minutes when the phone rang. My mom had shocking news. She said, "Your daddy is in intensive care." My husband and I drove to the hospital to see my daddy, maybe for the last time. My prayers began as we drove. I called my prayer chain at church and my prayer warrior friend. The prayers rose up to heaven asking for guidance and healing if it was the Father's will.

I later found out the details. In the middle of the night, Dad was rushed to the hospital. It was a frightening night for my mom. God's provision was there, and He was present all the time to help and assist her. When we look to see God's presence all around us, we realize He is never far away in times of trouble.

My mother's sister came to visit on Saturday at 3:00 p.m. Not so unusual, but these sisters had not seen each other for eighteen years. My dad became ill ten hours later. My aunt is a nurse and was there when my father passed out.

My mother, upset and frightened, called the ambulance. With tears in her eyes and a shaky voice, she called out for help. The person on the other end was gentle and calm. She was my mother's housekeeper who only worked at the ambulance service once a week, and this was her night to work. God provided a calm, loving, and familiar voice on the other end of the line. She talked to my mom till the ambulance arrived.

My aunt drove my mom to the hospital, following the ambulance, and stayed with her, assuring her things were going to be all right. She was there to take care of her sister when the rest of the family was out of town. When I walked into the intensive care unit to see my daddy, I knew he would recover because God gave me this assurance. I called my children and said, "Come and see your grandfather. He really looks bad but, he will be all right."

There were tubes coming from him, and he was swollen twice his normal size. He was unconscious and on a ventilator. The doctors gave us little hope. In my soul I knew he would be healed. I just needed to trust God with my daddy's life. We all needed to trust God with the outcome of this overwhelming time in our lives. God had my daddy's life right in the palm of His hand.

We tried not to live in the world of what ifs; we lived only in the moment we were in. Mom and I vowed not to cry unless we knew just why we were crying. Fear of the unknown can shake one's faith. We needed to pray for the future to be God's will. We needed to pray for strength, patience, endurance, and calmness. We needed to be in constant prayer.

The first week in the intensive care waiting room took its toll on us. Devastated people were all around my mom and me because their loved ones were sick or dying. I prayed and reached out to them with comfort and support. We stayed all the time the first week and then we went home only at nights.

Tough decisions were going to be made daily by my mom. She needed to trust God to direct her. The first week, a decision was made to give my dad a tracheotomy. He could not breathe on his own and was on a ventilator; the tracheotomy would help him. With this procedure he would not be able to speak on his own. We trusted God with this decision.

When we took our eyes off of Jesus, we felt like we were free falling off a cliff. When we focused on our situation, our emotions were on the surface and ready to consume our lives. There was total mental exhaustion because of the stress we were under. Letting God provide for us helped us get through each day, week after week.

In fifty-three days, God did a marvelous work in my daddy's life. He healed him and brought him from a place that looked like death. God restored his health and strength. God was in control and did not call my daddy home. He recovered when some people had given up hope for his life. God was in control.

Jesus was with my daddy during these fifty-three days. When it was all over and he was home, my pastor came to visit my dad while I was there. My dad told the pastor, "I never really believed everything the Bible said. But now I believe the Bible must be true." My dad still did not know Jesus as his savior but for the first time could read the Bible and believe the words in it. God provided for my mom and my daddy, and God was providing for the others in the waiting room of the hospital. God healed the sick and comforted the waiting.

I am thankful that God provided all our needs that day in August. He answered our prayers and restored my daddy's health in fifty-three days. But my dad was angry because he could no longer work or build like he wanted. He did not accept the fact he was growing old. I wondered why he couldn't understand; God had given him another chance to live. He really did not know how close to death he was. He believed the Bible to be true now, and I was thankful. I had prayed for my parents to go back to church for thirty-five years, and now my dad was going to go to church once more. I was still unsure about his salvation because believing the word of God is true and not knowing Jesus as your savior means your life is not truly the Lords.

In 2006, I walked with God. I was so glad I came to understand the beauty in death, as it would be all around me that year. Friday, January 6, I took my mom to the eye doctor to prepare for cataract surgery on Monday. She also was blind with an eye disease and could only see out of the sides of her eyes and not forward. We sat in the office waiting for the doctor when my mom held up two fingers in front of her and said, "I can see! Maybe I am getting better?" I said, "Mom, you are looking out of the sides of your eyes you are not looking forward. You have trained yourself to see forward by looking to your right." She said, "Does it look funny?" I said, "No, it looks alright."

On Sunday, I asked my husband to leave Sunday school early and go to pick up my mom while I sat at the retreat registration table that day. Gib forgot to pick her up, and when I got into the sanctuary, I saw he forgot her. I then went after her as they sang the first song. When I arrived at her house a few blocks from church, there was no answer at the door. When I went in, I called for her and there was no response. As I walked down the long hallway, I knew something was very wrong.

She was in bed and had gone to heaven, and she was looking to her right and smiling. What joy that brought me to see her looking to the right; I knew she was looking straight up to heaven. It was beautiful. I dropped to my knees and prayed to my God, thanking Him for my mother's life and for the love she had given me. After I prayed, I called 911. That was a great difference from the girl who wailed at a stranger's funeral. I knew God, and He knew me. How beautiful.

My boys and their families were all in church, and I was alone. I wanted to wait till church was over to call. I had left my phone in my purse by Gib on the pew and it rang. Scott grabbed it and left church to answer, no one was on the line. Scott knew something was wrong, so he called Grandma's house. I told him his grandma had died and asked him to send Gib and bring the pastor when church was over. Then I called my brother and Tim. When we looked later to see who called during church on my cell phone, the caller ID had no call at that time.

While I waited for my family to arrive, I went to my car and got a CD player and played Christian music to remind everyone when they arrived of God's loving presence. Gib and Christie were the first to arrive; the police, firemen, and coroner were no longer there. I took my husband and daughter-in-law back to my mom's bedroom and prayed with them with beautiful music in the background, thanking God for her life here on earth; they wept. Next Scott came, and I took him into the room and we prayed together.

My brother arrived. He cried while I prayed, but he never went back into the room with her. When Tim's church was over, I called him. He came alone, and I prayed with him. Then the pastor arrived. He gave a devotional and said prayers. He read from God's word, but my brother never entered the room; he stood in the hallway. When we were all done, the funeral home arrived to take my mother away. God was with us; the timing was perfect, and God was faithful.

My brother, David, was home for New Years and left to go home on the second of January, only to be called back on the eighth. While he was home, my father, who was living in assisted living and feeling lonely, called my mom on New Year's Eve and threatened to kill himself, which upset my mom. Although my dad believed the Bible to be true he did not know Jesus as his Lord and Savior. When I heard of my father's threats I called Rex, a Christian man I knew, and asked him to go by and tell my dad about how Jesus died for him on that cross and how by believing he would be saved. Rex was my dad's yardman and had spoken of Jesus often to my dad, but my dad never accepted that Jesus did that for him.

I told Rex on the third to go by and see my dad because of the suicide threats, but he couldn't get by right away. When he heard of mom's death on the eighth, Rex went to see my dad on the ninth. I didn't know Rex had talked to my dad, but when we wheeled Dad into the funeral home and up to Mom's casket for the first time, my dad stood up and raised his hands in the air and said, "There is a Jesus, and He saved me." This was what I prayed for, and my heart was at peace, for my dad was in such poor health too.

My father was living in a nursing home and was failing fast. I would watch him wither and die there in nine months. In July, six months after my mother died, my father's temperature dropped to eighty-seven degrees, and the nursing home rushed him to the hospital. He was not responsive; the doctor asked what his directive was. My father would never sign the directive. All he ever said was, "I want to live." When the doctors would ask me what his wishes were, I would say, "He wants to live." We spent a long day in intensive care with the doctors working on him for hours. The doctor brought my father back from the death that was to be his that day but at the end of the day he lived as he wished.

He was in the hospital a while, then returned to the nursing home, never to get out of bed again on his own. He could never feed himself, roll over, or stand again. But he could talk and smile, and he knew what was going on around him. He appreciated little things like Oreo cookies and Snickers bars. It was not time for him to go home yet; it was his second brush with death. He was a warrior in death, brave and unafraid. In October, my father was very bad. We were waiting day-by-day for him to join my mom in heaven.

On Sunday, October 15, at 5:00 a.m., the phone rang. I knew it must be time for my father to leave; the nurses had warned us it could be any time. The doctor on the other end said, "We have your brother David here in Florida. He is in a coma, his brain is swelling, and there is no response; he is on a ventilator. He has a large mass on the front two lobes of his brain, and there is little hope." Wow!

My brother was forty-four years old, sixteen years younger than me. This was the baby I took care of when I was a teenager, the one I mothered like my own, and the one who wanted to live with me when I married. I prayed for my brother and my father; they were both getting ready for the journey home.

On Wednesday, my brother went to heaven while in the hospital in Florida. I brought him back to Cape, and he was buried next to my mom on Saturday. I told my dad that David would be seeing him soon, and he smiled. I never told him he died.

In the evening, after my brother's funeral, we went out to dinner with some of my brother's friends who were still in town. I was sitting by my brother Dan when the phone rang; it was the nursing home. Dan looked at me, and we knew we were not ready for another death today.

Two days later, about noon, we got the call we expected, and my father was passing. God is everywhere, if we just look to see where he is in all situations. This was the third time my father was close to death, and this time God was calling him home. We went to be with my dad, and I played soft praise music during the day as we waited. As my dad's body failed him, I told him my mom wanted him to come and join her and that she had a big surprise for him when he got there. (It was David, but my dad still did not know he died.)

I find beauty in death because God is always there. My son Tim and his family were the last to arrive that Monday. He held his little three-year-old daughter by Grandpa's bedside. She began to sing, "Jesus Loves Me" to Grandpa. When she was done, Tim put her down and she walked over to her mom, and my father went to heaven. Beautiful.

I had planned my dad's funeral a week before David died, and now I was to plan another. While David was in the hospital with no response, I planned his funeral too. I got matching caskets; my dad's more regal than David's. I didn't know if there would be a double funeral or not. The relatives were all there for David's funeral on Saturday, and then came back on Tuesday for my Dad's.

A friend of my brothers brought all David's ties when he arrived for the funeral. I put an *I Love Lucy* tie on David. It had her face with a big smile and bright eyes on it. David was known for his unusual ties. I gave all the relatives a tie to remember David and his humorous personality. In his casket with him was a Garfield cat. When he was home on New Years, he saw this cat at the Airport gift shop. He said the cat looked alone after Christmas, and he felt sad for the cat, so he bought him.

I planned the funeral service with my pastor and wrote a note about my brother on the back of the folder; it read:

One Special Brother

Let me tell you about my brother David. He was a sweet little boy who loved his mom and dad. He was always good and so smart. He knew the states and capitals of the states at the age of four. He could read in kindergarten. All his teachers loved him; some still ask about him today.

When he was born, he had a sixteen-year-old sister and an eighteen-year-old brother. Sometimes he seemed older than them. When he was three years old, Patty got married, and he thought he was moving with her into her new trailer. What a let down.

When David was four years old, he moved into an apartment with Mom, Dad, Danny, and Honey, the collie dog, while the home in the country was being built. What noisy group for a little apartment. Dan got married while in the apartment, then David and his parents moved to the country where he lived till he moved on to college.

David always loved animals and he had Mac, the Dalmatian, and Katie, the German Shepard, during his life in the country. David grew to be a cat lover because of his many apartments during his writing career. He left his best friend, Hairy the cat, in Florida with four other cats and a dog; they will miss him now.

As a child, David traveled all over the world with his parents and on his own as a young man. He got to see so much of the world and gained great knowledge that would help him later in his life. David became Dave the writer after he attended college at Westminster in Fulton, Missouri. He went to Washington University for a semester. He even traveled with the late Congressman Bill Emerson as he toured his district. He loved politics as a young man.

Then he began writing for newspapers, magazines, and wrote freelance columns. He traveled from Chicago to Florida, and many places in between, writing. He was a man of many words but always had deep roots for his home and parents. He would call every Sunday evening just to hear Mom's voice. She was his greatest fan and confidant.

My brother was a great writer and humorist. He could find humor in everything around him and wrote about it. All the relatives know how he would share jokes by phone or e-mail frequently. He had a lot of laughter around him and lived life in his way with joy and laughter surrounding him. David, or Dave, as he liked to be called now, lived to write about his passions and wrote in his own unique way. He was a man who took pride in his work and always gave more than required to his job.

If you knew him, you were very fortunate if you were his friend; he never forgot you through his letters, birthday cards, and e-mails. If you were Dave's friend once, you are still part of his life. Dave had such love for his friends and showed it. He had a lot of love to share and had a lot of friends to give that love to. If you were his relative, you loved him because he was a very special person with a personality of his own. He was always drawn to his parents with a deep bond of devotion and love.

Remember, David won't be far away; we always have his writings to hear his voice again. And if you listen within your heart, you willknow his love all around you. Celebrate his life; don't grieve his death, and never forget his sweet spirit of love and devotion. Let God heal your grieving heart and hold you in His mighty arms as you learn to live life without the presence of David John Wiethop.

Tears still fill my eyes when I read about the brother who should still be here, but God has called him home before me. I don't understand the way things happen, but I trust God with all things. God was faithful to bring me through 2006. My faith grew stronger, and I realized God is in control.

Now, I had a big hole in my heart, and I needed someone to help fill that gap, someone to love me and care for me unconditionally.

My Doggy

We always said we would get a dog when Gib retired. Maybe a Yorkie, they were small. Then our friends got a Pomeranian; his name was Sammy, he was golden in color and so cute. What I liked best was how he turned his head from side to side as if he really understood every word I was saying to him. I told him I was his Grammy, and he would cock his head as if to say, "I know."

Our dog would be golden and a male like Sammy. Our dog would be the size of Sammy, about eight or so pounds and cute just like Sammy and we would call him Banjo.

Gib was about two and a half years from retirement, so we planned that in the summer of 2009 we would get our golden, male Pomeranian. It is strange how sometimes our plans get changed when times of trouble arrive. In 2006, when my mom, dad, and brother died, I was very sad. The cloud of mourning hung over me. Dogs fill the void in our lives, and boy did I have a void. Dogs are faithful and loyal and loving. Dogs love unconditionally, and I needed all of these things in my life right then.

About three weeks after the last death, I told Gib, "I need a dog, now!" He agreed, and I called my niece who worked for a vet in a nearby town. She gave me a name of a breeder. I called to see if they had any dogs. The breeder's name was Toni, and she said, "Yes, we have two, and they are four months old and ready to go." We went to see the pups the next day, and there was the love of my life. She was all black, not a speck of color anywhere. I said, "I want that one." Toni said, "I really don't want to sell the all black one, I have tried to breed a solid black one for years. I went to Tennessee where her sire was a solid black show dog and has won ribbons in many shows. No, I don't want to sell that one."

The feelings of loss started to arise, but this black dog's sister had white down both sides and had white on her paws. She was cute too. She was not the one that caught my eye, but we bought her anyway. I said I would pick her up in one week when we returned from a vacation we had planned. When we arrived home from our trip, there was a message on the answering machine asking us if we wanted the solid black female dog. I called Toni, and she said she had a buyer for her sister and because I was the first with the money, I had first pick. "Yes. Oh Yes! I want the black one," I said.

I took my girlfriend, Martha, along to pick her up and Martha held her all the way home. My new little doggy was going home and her Aunt Martha held her in a new little pink baby blanket. I did not realize how much this little dog would help me to mourn the loss of my family and how much she would love me unconditionally.

I believe this little doggy saved my life. I now had someone to give all the love I had stored up. The love for my mom, my dad, and my brother that I could no longer give to them was now going to be given to my little doggy.

I named my new doggy CC's Banjo Anne of Editors Black Ink, a big name for a wee little dog. The CC came from Banjo's mother, her name is Candy Cane, and my father's initials were CC. I named her Banjo because my living brother plays the banjo, and my mom's name was Anne. Banjo's father's name is Editors Black Ink and my deceased brother was an editor of a newspaper. This little doggy had my family's name and I knew I was going to give all my lost love to her, my CC's Banjo Anne of Editor's Black Ink, or Banjo for short.

When Banjo was four months old, she weighed one and a half pounds; now she weighs three. She is very small and just fits on your lap to pet and hold perfectly. She is a faithful dog and loves me. She would lie by my side as I stroked her black hair and cried for my parents while I mourned. We never played much, just sat and loved one another. Now when she plays, she plays by herself. She runs up and down the halls and into the rooms throwing her toys into the air, and if I try to join in, she stops and looks at me as if to say, "What are you doing? I'm playing."

I taught her to travel in a purse and sit in a car seat in the car. She never barks when she is in her purse, so she shops with me. She goes where I go and loves it. She doesn't leave our yard when she is let out, and she sleeps by our bed on the end table in her small crate.

In 2008, I had a car wreck and was in the bed for eight weeks, and then for the next four months learned to walk on my own. My little dog was faithful. She lay in bed with me for hours and never left my side. She knew I needed her to love me, so I would not be sad lying there for so long. The year of my car wreck, I couldn't walk and had to keep my foot elevated. I went to a Halloween Party in a wheelchair and dressed like a beekeeper. I had a red box on my lap that said "Killer Bee." When the costume judging came later in the evening, I opened the lid of the box and there was Banjo dressed in a bee costume; we won a prize. This year, I entered Banjo in a nursing home Halloween costume contest. She was a ballerina and won doggy treats and a certificate for best dressed.

Banjo is very patient with me. She just loves me so much, she will put up with anything. When we are at the lake, she rides in the golf cart with us in the back bucket behind the seat. I could not have found a better doggy for me. A dog I can buy clothes for and dress up; a dog that I can take along in my purse. My husband loves this little doggy too. Banjo brings such joy to our family. I know that dogs bring joy because Banjo is a qualified Pet Pal. She goes into nursing homes and hospitals to visit the patients. Their eyes light up when they see this small little doggy prancing down the hallways with a bow around her neck.

One day, we went into the Alzheimer's unit, and there was a lady trying to eat an ice cream with a spoon, but she forgot how to use the spoon. I walked up to her and held my dog up so she could see her. The lady put her ice cream down and put her hands up to her own cheeks with an expression of amazement; her eyes lit up and she said, "Doggy!"

When I am longing for my family and sad, I hug my doggy and stroke her beautiful black hair and know I can give all the love I had for them to this little doggy and she will respond with love. She is so faithful to me that when I leave one room in the house and go to another, I just look around and there will be Banjo lying somewhere by my side. She never leaves me alone.

The ability to love was instilled in us by God. Even people who do not know Jesus can love their parents and family, all of us have it. When loved ones die, the pain of loss is so great. If we give our love for them away, the pain is less. I thank God for my Banjo.

JAMES 3:16

"Where there is jealousy and selfishness there
is also disorder and every kind of evil."

Jealousy, selfishness, disorder and every kind of evil, sounds like the
sin the Bible describes many time. The Bible tells us not to sin and
these are just a few of the sins the Bible talks about. Sin separates
us from God and when we are out of God's presence, evil can dwell.

Is that a description of your life? Are you living outside of the
dwelling place God has made for you? Step back and take a good
look at your life. Is your life pleasing to God the way it is? What
changes need to take place in your life today? Call upon the Lord's
strength to help you overcome the sin in it. Where are you headed?
Is sin in control of your destiny? Call upon the name of the Lord
Jesus Christ and He will forgive you and save you.

THE REALITY OF GOD

This chapter of writings is about God and His presence in our lives. He is real and is in the midst of all things. People live as if God were somewhere else and not with them, but He is always with us as the word says.

Forgiveness

The word forgiveness is a very difficult word. It is hard for us to forgive and hard to accept forgiveness because we want to hold on to our anger. We want to have our own way and stay angry, yet we don't realize how our anger affects us. How should we live in an angry world? How should we react when people retaliate against us? These are questions asked every day.

We say, "I have a right to be angry, to hold a grudge," even if the offense happened years ago. We say, "Well, maybe I'll forgive them but I could never forget what they did to me." Our hearts turn cold with an unforgiving spirit. Our sin separates us from God.

There was a man who was angry with his own brother for sixty years. He believed he should have the family farm. When he did not get the farm and his brother got to live there instead, he stayed mad at his own brother for sixty years. Family feuds happen all the time over possessions. And people within families do not speak to one another for years.

In our world, people hold on to anger like it is a precious gem to cling to and to protect. They did me wrong, they deserved it, I'll get even with them over this. Statements like these just add fuel to the fire burning inside. The anger grows and it gets harder to let go and forgive. God is the only way to eliminate an unforgiving spirit. Look to His word for guidance and see what the Master says in Ephesians 4:32,

> Be kind and compassionate to one another, forgiving each other, just as in Christ God forgave you.
>
> Ephesians 4:32

To our enemies we are to be kind and tenderhearted, it plainly says to forgive one another. The word of God always directs us to the way we should live. We read in Matthew;

> For if you forgive men when they sin against you, your heavenly Father will also forgive you.
>
> Matthew 6:14

This verse is a directive to us. We must forgive others. Does God know just how hard that can be? Our God sent His son to die for us to forgive us. He isn't asking for our son. He is asking us to release our sin of unforgiveness to Him because His Son has already died for us. God does not want to be separated from you and me. He just loves us too much. No matter what we do to offend the Almighty and everlasting God of this universe, He forgives us because Christ came to earth for us so we would not be offensive to God.

> For as high as the heavens are above the earth, so great is His love for those who fear Him; as far as the east is from the west, so far has He removed our transgressions from us.
>
> Psalm 103:11–12

We can hardly comprehend what God has truly done for us because He has not only forgiven us; he has removed our sin as far as the east is from the west. Just think, when you go east you never meet west, but when you go north long enough you start going south. As far as the east is from the west is never-ending.

Jeremiah 31:34 b says,

> For I will forgive their wickedness and will remember their sin no more.
>
> Jeremiah 31:34b

God is faithful and has promised to remember our sin no more. We find it hard to accept God's forgiveness. We cannot forgive ourselves. We beat ourselves up over poor choices and mistakes. We can barely exist at times because we think we are so undeserving of any forgiveness and we cling to our guilt. The way human beings deal with forgiveness is a poor example of how our Heavenly Father teaches us. We should be praising such a loving God who promised to forget past sins and make us new. We need to know what God's Holy Word teaches us about His loving mercy. The scripture says,

> If I had cherished sin in my heart, the Lord would not have listened; but God has surely listened and heard my voice in prayer. Praise be to God, who has not rejected my prayer or withheld His love from me!
>
> Psalm 66:18–20

God will forgive us and will hear our prayers because He loved us while we were yet sinners. God has such mercy and love for His people that he overlooks our flaws and calls us to come to Him. We are truly not deserving of this kind of love. We have Christ's spirit in us, and we have the power to forgive and forget. We can even forgive ourselves with Christ living in us, and we no longer need to beat ourselves up over our past. This doesn't make sense. It isn't our *lives* that love one another it's *us*. And we no longer hold others accountable for poor behavior toward us. We are free from being enslaved by the sin of an unforgiving heart.

We need to cling to the words of blessings from God in Psalm 32:1–2,

> Blessed is he whose transgression is forgiven, whose sins are covered. Blessed is the man whose sin the Lord does not count against him and in whose spirit is no deceit.
>
> Psalm 32:1–2

Reunions

My first pastor was in town today; he is my spiritual father, the one who told me about Jesus my Savior. He is still telling me about God and Christ's indwelling spirit. He is still speaking of forgiveness, because Jesus died for me. This weekend was a time of affirmation of faith. I know on my own I can do nothing worthwhile, but with Christ living in me, I can be used by God. God uses me; He prepares my heart and puts people in my path. He fills me with the desire to tell others about Jesus' saving grace. I am urged to witness for Christ. I am excited about the Savior who saved me, and I feel like I would explode if I don't tell others.

Every morning I thank God for allowing me one more day here on this earth to share the knowledge of Christ with others. I always say, "Use me, Lord, I am willing." I will cancel all my plans for the day if God calls me elsewhere. When people need me, I am willing to give them as much of my time as they need. God wants us to be like Jesus, so we are to listen to others and help them. When I think of someone, I call or go by to see him or her. I might write someone a note, but I act upon the thought. I want to tell others about my Savior and am bold in my faith only because I understand that the Holy Spirit of God lives in me. I do not speak on my own but by the power of the Holy Spirit. God provides my words to speak and my heart to love. I have compassion to understand others' needs because of that same Spirit.

The time is short, and the message is needed throughout the land. We are to bring love to a world that does not know Him. There is nothing more important than the knowledge of Christ. We are to go where we are sent and love all people enough to tell them the wonderful news of the risen Christ. I thank God for my first pastor because without Him, I may not have come to know Jesus as my Savior. Reunions are times to remember and rejoice.

They Call Me Teacher

I couldn't believe what I heard! They called me teacher! The girls in jail said I was the best Bible teacher they ever had. All I did was drive to Jackson, pray, and then I went into the jail, and they locked the doors behind me. Then we talked, and God's Holy Spirit did the rest. It was truly awesome to be there as a witness to the working of the Holy Spirit. I ask myself, me a teacher? No, God was the teacher. I was the instrument that He used this evening.

I truly want to serve the Lord, but I am sick and fragile. I have no strength, no physical endurance. But God is mighty and powerful, strong and wise. The Bible talks about putting on the new nature and taking off the old. Well, the old nature in me is full of sin and despair, but the new nature is the nature of God.

When I came to know God gave up His son for me so I could live, His Holy Spirit came into my life. I didn't really know what to do at first, so I continued living the only way I knew. But God was patient and forgiving to me, and He waited. He waited until I cried out for His help, and then He was there. I started my walk with Jesus as my guide. I needed to get close to God and learn of the power He has given me through His spirit.

I am maturing every day, coming closer to God, relying on God, and trusting in God. My life now is worth nothing without God. My old nature is useless, but my new nature in Christ has awesome power. As I teach through the Holy Spirit, God gives me the wisdom it takes to share His truths.

Tonight we read from Colossians.

> Set your minds on things above, not on earthly things.
> Colossians 3:2

One girl was going to rehabilitation this week. She has a choice to make. Will she live for Christ or will she live for herself, it is her choice. Will she please God or please man? Tonight was her time to call upon Christ so the peace of Christ could rule in her heart. The Bible promised that the word of Christ would dwell in her richly if she claims that promise from God. I don't know what her future holds, but God almighty does hold her future.

I could never be a teacher on my own merit. But with God, anything is truly possible. Yes, oh yes, I am a teacher through Christ Jesus.

> Let the word of Christ dwell in you richly as you teach and admonish one another with all wisdom, and as you sing psalms, hymns and spiritual songs with gratitude in your hearts to God.
> Colossians 3:16

Yes, I am God's teacher with the help of God.

Light the Fire

Satan was working overtime this week. He was doing everything he could to keep people away from the Show Me Center in Cape Girardeau. God is Great, Jesus is Lord, and the Holy Spirit was at the Show Me Center for eight days in March.

This was the first evangelist's crusade since 1926, when Bill Sunday was here. Lowell Lundstrum was his name. He and his team traveled 300 days a year. They tell people about Jesus. They dedicate themselves to Christ, and Satan scrambled to stand in the way so people couldn't get to the crusade. He whispered lame excuses in their ears and they didn't come. I wondered what could be more important than Jesus? I asked people to hear about Jesus, and they acted like I asked them to visit some heathen place. Some were afraid of being seen there. I guess they thought they would get a bad name.

Fourteen thousand weren't ashamed of the gospel. Fourteen thousand were sent to come one night or another. This was not about a cult; this was about the gospel of Jesus Christ. Satan had a lot of trouble shutting the doors of their hearts.

Gib and I couldn't stay away; it was an experience of singing and praising with thousands of other believers. Lowell's messages were strong and affirming, and each night we learned more about Jesus and longed to serve Him more. It changed my life; I learned what God expects of me and how much He loves me. There were twenty-eight hours of praise and worship as we learned to know Jesus more.

Why wouldn't they come? This was a time for God's church to unite in one body and declare that Jesus is Lord. Sixty area churches of all denominations gathered with us each night. Lowell spoke about salvation through Christ's death and resurrection and about forgiveness and sins. He spoke plainly and clearly every night.

Saturday night, at the end of the evening, Lowell called a man to the stage. The man seemed so strong, his voice didn't even quiver. This man spoke about his thirteen-year-old daughter who was at the crusade every night in the front row. She was in love with Jesus, and she shared this with everyone she met. At 12:30 p.m. that very afternoon, Sandy, at the age of thirteen, was in a car wreck with her mother and tonight her father said, "Sandy died and went home to Jesus today," it was in a moment and his heart was rejoicing. His wife lay in the hospital, his daughter lay in the funeral home, and he came to praise his

Lord Jesus and thank Him for his family. Tonight, he sat in the front row praising and worshipping with his six other children by his side; they didn't want to be anywhere else.

The Holy Spirit was in that very room. He must have found comfort when Lowell spoke about our names being recorded in the lamb's book of life, knowing Sandy's was there.

People were on fire for Jesus all over the Show Me Center this week. I was in a room full of happy Christians. When I went to my church the next week, a few people were happy, some were sad, and you could see it, some were just there because. Our pastor was full of God's Spirit, and in his sermon he spoke of joy. He was very joyful, but not many of the faces changed. What can we do to light the fire in their hearts? The fire will help them seek after God's word then they will pray more, and love the Lord enough to tell others about His grace. I pray the burning embers of their hearts could be stirred enough to light the flame in their hearts. Smoldering coals don't set fires, but they do eventually burn out.

I want the people in the pews to be bold in spirit, smiling and praising Jesus. I want them to be proud to be a Christian, telling everyone of Christ's sacrifice for us. We learn from the Spirit of God how to live and how to be bold in faith.

This was a glorious week full of love, peace, and joy. I pray Christians can make an impact on America and show how good and how gracious God is. Everyone involved in this event gave praise to God for the people who came to know the Lord Jesus for the first time. Hundreds heard that Jesus Christ died on the cross just for them to be forgiven. People learned eternal life was theirs, and they would live forever with God through His Son Jesus.

I prayed every day for the crusade to be all God intended it to be, and it was greater and grander then I could imagine. God lit fires this week at the Show Me Center. He renewed spirits, mended hearts, gave wisdom to His children, and gave new birth to many. It is not because of Lowel Lundstrum, but because of the Holy Sprit's presence.

Face-to-Face

Carla Faye Tucker is sentenced to die today for her crime of murder. She beat to death a human being with a bat. Such a terrible crime! But fourteen years ago behind those bars, Carla accepted God's gift of grace for her. She repented of her sins and asked for forgiveness. God is so almighty he changed the life of a drug-obsessed, hard-hearted murderer. Carla Faye Tucker's name was written in God's book of life. She witnessed for Christ for fourteen years while in prison, and today is the last day for her to tell of God's grace through Jesus' death and how God loves all people.

I don't know as of right now just what will happen today. But, I do know whatever it is, it is God's will. Carla is so fortunate to be looking toward death with a Savior for her soul. I am so happy that during the last fourteen years she knew Jesus as her Savior. She was made new and changed, and I praise God for that.

Every day I think about Jesus returning and my being with Him forever, but what if I die before His return? I pray that when I die, I will die talking about Jesus. I want to be telling others about Him and His promises of salvation for His people. One moment, I will be singing praises of Him, and the next moment, I'd be singing to Him in his presence.

God's word promises me I will be complete when I meet Him face-to-face. How grand that day will be. Carla knows just when she will meet Him face-to-face; it will be at 6:00 p.m. today. She will have no memory of that old person with the stone heart who lived for drugs and the things of the world. Today she will be with Him in paradise. Death is not so sad when you know that your future is to be face-to-face, truly in the presence of the Living God. That will be better than anything I could ever imagine. I long to meet Him, to see His face, to praise Him, and worship Him always and forever. While I stay here, I will worship Him and sing praises to Him. I want to bring glory to Him through my obedience and love. Every day I want to tell everyone about Jesus or reassure His children of His love. I want to guide them in the way they should go. I pray when I meet Him face-to-face, when it's my time to go, when I am called or when He comes for me in the clouds, at that very moment, I pray my lips will be speaking His name.

Maybe Carla's life was not a testimony fifteen year ago, but God can do powerful things. Her life changed, and you can see the power of God as she served Him in prison. Her new life as a witness to all who knew what she did and how she lived before, and now she is a testimony of God's saving grace.

I know all Christians have this as their hearts cry when they meet Him face-to-face. Have you served Him since you've known Him? One day we will see Him face-to-face, and it may be sooner than you've planned.

So I Wait

I'm waiting for you. You said you would come back. I look for you every day. I love you so much. You promised me you would return, and I believe you, so I wait.

Every day I wait. Will today be the day, or will it be tomorrow? Please come back, I need you. I want to be with you. I love you. You mean everything to me.

This sounds like a child calling to her father who has left her. Oh, the emptiness she must feel. The longing she has to be with him. Oh, how much love she must feel for her father. It is about a child and her father. The child is myself and .my Jesus is God. I love Him...father, and I wait for Jesus's return every day. He says He will meet me in the clouds. Oh, how I long for that day. I look into the clouds everyday with expectation of His return.

Maybe He won't come in my lifetime, but He will come in someone's. So I wait. I'm ready to go. My bags are packed, and I wait. I have Jesus as my Savior. I know He hung on that cross for my sins, and I know I'm free. I am free from the penalty of death and separation from God. I am saved and will be joined together with Him in heaven, forever. So I wait.

Are you ready today for His return? Will you meet Him in the sky? God alone knows your heart and your mind. Is your heart His? Is your mind set on heavenly things? Is Jesus your Savior? Do you mean it? Do you really, really mean it? God knows. Look, and watch for His return.

Look, He is coming with the clouds, and every eye will see Him, even those who pierce Him; and all the people of the earth will mourn because of Him. So it shall be! Amen.

Revelation 1:7

At that time men will see the Son of Man coming in the clouds with great power and glory, and He will send His angels and gather His elect from the four winds, from the ends of the earth to the ends of the heavens.

Mark 13:26–27

After that, we who are still alive and are left will be caught up together with them in the clouds to meet the Lord in the air. And so we will be with the Lord forever.

1 Thessalonians 4:7

Are you ready? Are you watching? Are you waiting? Look up. He may be coming.

The End

Sometimes I am puzzled when people want to know when the end of time is coming. Why do they want to know? Is it so they can do better, or is it so they can get closer to God? Maybe it is to complete some unfinished task. Or maybe it is to just get right! Some people seem frightened about the end and Christ coming again. They seem concerned about the tribulation and if they'll be strong enough when it comes. My puzzlement comes because my last day on this earth may be today. I may never see Christ's coming again in glory, so why worry?

I believe God's promises that He will never leave me nor forsake me. Seems pretty simple, but that's my faith, just simple, no rules, just faith in God. If I live till the tribulation of this world's end time, or just my own life's tribulation, I know God will protect me, and my faith will be strong. I know through His promises I will have peace, joy, and love from my Father in heaven.

This place called earth is not such a wonderful place. There are heartaches everywhere. We have divorce, hatred, selfishness, greed, power, envy, immorality, and the list goes on and on. If I look at the good things around me there are many gifts from God. I see God in the mountains, streams, flowers, birds, babies, music, and many, many gifts. All these gifts bring us love, joy, and peace. God's intent was to save all His children from death and separation from Him.

> Trust in the Lord with all your heart.
>
> Proverbs 3:5

This verse I hold very dear.

So! What about the end times? There are no end times for those who love the Lord and believe in Him. We are only in a holding pattern waiting for our landing in heaven. How could our life on earth be all there is when we are only here less than a hundred years? God has a better place prepared for us.

When trials hit our lives, will we be strong enough? Certainly, through Christ Jesus we can do anything. The Bible says,

> And the Peace of God, which transcends all understanding, will guard your hearts and minds in Christ Jesus.
>
> Philippians 4:7

On my own I can do nothing. When will the end come? It will come in God's time. What can I do? Nothing, God will do everything that needs to be done.

I remember when Iben Browning, a local man, predicted an earthquake for December 3rd in our community. Everyone wanted to believe a mere man, who could predict what God is doing. Everyone prepared and bought extra blankets, garbage cans filled with candles, distilled water, batteries, etc. Some people even left town on that day, they ran to hide and avoid injury from the quake. Where was their faith? They had faith that Ivan Browning was right. God's word says,

> Never will I leave you; never will I forsake you.
>
> Hebrews 13:5

Did they put their faith in the Lord or Browning?

Someone asked me what I was doing to prepare for the big quake! I told them, "I am praying more and studying God's word." I know no man can predict what God will do. He has His plans, and we cannot change them. God tells us how He wants us to act, and we can't even do that to His expectations. So they search the scriptures so they can be the one person on the earth who knows God's plans for the universe.

Instead of seeking the end, spend your time telling people about how good God is and how much He loves them, because He sent His Son to die on the cross in their place. Let us all live in the present and love one another. Our future is for God alone to know, so trust Him with your life.

2 THESSALONIANS 3:16

"Now may the Lord of peace himself give you peace at
all times and in every way? The Lord is with you."

God alone is the peace giver. God wants everyone to have peace at
all times, the kind of peace that dwells inside of your very being.
God wants to give you peace in every way. So many people live
separated from peace. Their lives reflect crisis. When there is the
absence of peace there could be the absence of the peace giver. Are
you walking with God or just believing there is a God? Is He your
help in times of trouble? Does He have prominence in your life?
God wants His right place in your heart. He wants a dwelling place.
Invite Him to come and dwell in you. Then you too can have peace
from the true peace giver.

SERVING GOD

I began living for the Lord after being ill; He became the only reason I had to live. Before I came to know Jesus, one night the phone rang in the hallway, and I had to get up and answer it. I was so sleepy and stumbled to the phone. When I answered it, it was a young man on the other end, he said, "Sharon, I can't live without you, I am going to kill myself." In my sleepiness, I answered saying, "I'm sorry you have the wrong number," and hung up the phone. The moment I hung up, I realized the desperate man on the other end said he was going to kill himself. I was so worried about him, I watched the papers to see if a young man died that week. Guilt came upon me, and for years I regret not speaking to that young man. Now I know to speak to all who call.

I was willing to do whatever God wanted me to do. So I watched and waited for the opportunity to serve others and to tell them about Jesus. I felt like God's ambassador, someone who would tell others about the great God we all have. I seemed to feel better when I was serving the Lord. My life changed dramatically after I became ill.

I began attending Christian Women's Club, a part of Stonecroft Ministries, and started teaching their Bibles Studies all over town. I had them in my home and then branched out to the community at Senior Centers, a shelter for battered women, a half way house for addicts, a homeless shelter, I held them in the parks and in ladies homes with their friends. I went to the city jail and the county jail to teach. Sometimes I would teach one on one with anyone who wanted to know more about the Lord. As I followed God and was always willing to serve, He led me to teach. Some weeks I would teach five or more classes. I was blessed by His word, and I was willing to tell others about the Savior of the world, Jesus.

I found myself counseling people with their problems. God used me, and I was more than willing. One day, a neighbor girl stopped by on a school day. She never stopped before, but I knew her. I think she was running away from home that day. We talked for hours about her life and the Lord. She was confused and lost, but that day she left knowing more about Jesus. There was the lady who was walking around the neighborhood asking for money. We talked about Jesus for a long time, and He blessed her before she left. She was going back to church because she remembered her first love.

Sometimes my sons' friends would come over to talk to me about their lives, and I would listen to them and tell them about Jesus. Brandon was leading a life full of sex and drugs that would only harm him; we would talk for hours in my office. He did not want to live the way he was living but did not know a way out of his circumstances.

He was kicked out of high school and tossed around by his divorced parents; he felt unworthy and unwanted. He led a life that was destructive to him. I didn't know if Brandon knew the Lord as his Savior when he left town to live with his grandparents, but years later Brandon returned to Cape and came to see me. He wanted to tell me he knew Jesus as his Savior and thank me for all the hours we spent talking about Jesus in my office.

Girls and guys came into my home during the time my boys were teens. We spent hours talking about how to live their lives pleasing to God; I was their Christian counselor. We talked about their sex lives and how casual it was for them, and we talked about self-respect. We talked about God, and His plan for their lives. My home was a place the kids liked to hang out. Even after they were out of high school, our place was the place to be. They are now adults with children of their own and are good parents and spouses.

Whenever God called upon me, I would go and help someone; I never questioned His call. One day Kathy just stopped by my home. I knew her casually, and she had never stopped before. She asked me if I would go visit her stepbrother in the hospital who was dying. He was only her stepbrother for a few weeks because her dad got a divorce. Marriage never works when there are two alcoholics under the same roof. Her stepbrother was raised with alcoholism all around him and began drinking at an early age. Now he was twenty and was an alcoholic. She said he looked a little rough. I did not know what that meant, but I went to the hospital to see him, a perfect stranger.

The young man could not read or write and had tattoos all over his arms of satanic symbols. He was handsome for a young man with death all over his arms. We talked about how God loves him and how Satan can't have him if he belongs to God. His liver was failing, and if he drank again, it could kill him. While I was there, God sent a man in that brought a Bible on tape for this young man to hear God's word. He was so thankful for the man who brought him the words of God because he could not read. After a while, he became weary, and I said I would be back the next day. I got there the next morning, and the housekeeper was stripping his bed. I asked her where the young man went who had this room, but she did not know. I left knowing that God was watching over him and never saw him again.

We need to look to see where God is when we are called upon. He is always in the middle of everything. He prearranges all things. It is never an accident when things happen; God is in control of it all. When we realize that there are divine appointments, we will service the call quicker. I know I am not compassionate enough to serve others on my own. God is calling us all to go to His people and show our compassion to them. He arranges who needs us; we need to act upon the call.

The first Stonecroft Bible study I attended, the leader asked if I would like to lead a study; I said I would. The next week I went to the house of a Korean lady. She did not know the Lord as her Savior because she was a Buddhist. She was curious about Jesus. There were two other women at this study: Mary, who was a Christian, and an excommunicated Catholic lady who was disappointed in God for being kicked out of church. We met for years at this study; the two ladies came to have a personal relationship with Jesus. Because of this, the Korean lady's whole family came to know Jesus, and they will all spend eternity in heaven together.

I attended Bible Study Fellowship for years and one day a lady called me asking me if I could lead a bible study with a Jewish lady. She was hard to get along with and needed a one-on-one class situation, not a group. She was angry because her mother gave her away to an orphan's home at the age of five because of finances. She recalls her mother holding her hand as she walked across the street to be left at the orphan's home forever. When she grew up, she had an abusive marriage but had nine children from this union. She was angry and bitter about her life. God began a good work in her, and you could see the difference when she accepted Jesus as her Savior. She became a sweet little lady. She was a good friend, and we talked about Jesus and how He loves us all the time. I went to her home for years, and we studied the Bible together.

I called her to go to church with me on Ash Wednesday. When we got to church, a lady I played bridge with, named Judy, was there with another woman; they sat across the aisle from us. When church was over, we all met in the aisle. I introduced my friend to Judy, and she introduced her friend, Yarka, to us. Yarka was from the Czech Republic. She was in Cape Girardeau visiting relatives, and Judy was her English teacher.

Judy took me to the side and asked if I still taught Bible studies. I said, "Yes." Judy said, "Yarka wants to know about Jesus." I turned to Yarka and said, "Yarka, I heard you want to know about Jesus? Would you like to come to my house next Tuesday, and we can learn about Him?" She said yes. We met for six weeks, and on Easter Sunday, Yarka Dugava from the Czech Republic, got baptized at Hanover Lutheran Church. She went back to the Czech Republic three days later. Yarka and I still communicate by e-mail and she has been back to see me in Cape three times since then.

What if I did not heed the call when asked if I would teach a Bible study for these ladies? What if I just ignored the call and did my own thing? I gave up some time because of my love for my Lord. I was blessed by doing God's will and others were blessed to know Jesus.

I was asked to substitute at a Bible study in another town, and I said I would go. There were about seven ladies in this study, but that night no one showed up except the hostess. I did the study anyway. I was there just at the right time; God's time is perfect. The hostess began to cry and tell me about her two-year-old who had been run over by a friend who backed out of her driveway. She was still very sad even though it happened a few years ago. She had been shutting God out of her life and was angry with Him. That night changed her life as she came to love the Lord once more. She realized God was with her all along and loved her so much that he gave up his only Son for her. I did not get discouraged because no one arrived; I did the study anyway knowing God plans everything in advance.

I sold Avon for twenty-eight years, and one of my customers, Sharon, called me to tell me not to call her any more about ordering because her cancer had returned after many years. It was in her throat, and her voice box was going to be removed. The next week, I got a call from a nurse in the hospital where Sharon was, and she wrote a note telling the nurse to call me and give me her son's phone number asking me to call her there. I called the son the next week, and he said, "Mom wants you to come and see her." I did not know why she would want to see me, she was just a customer, but I went. I took some Christian books and the Bible to read to her, knowing we would have trouble communicating with each other. I read to her and sat with her the first day, and she asked me to come back, so I went back many times. When she got on her feet and began chemo and voice therapy, she would come to my home for Bible study every week. She learned to talk with a little machine held to her throat. She came to my home to study God's word for about two years while the cancer was in remission.

One day I got a call from her pastor, and he said she wanted him to call me and tell me the cancer had returned and to pray for her that evening because she would tell her children. The doctor gave her two months to live without chemo and six months to live with chemo. She made a decision not to have chemo again.

I wanted to go to her home to see her, but I didn't know what to say to a dying woman. I asked my pastor to go with me the first time because I felt I did not have the gift of mercy, and he could help me. We went and on the way home the pastor told me he experienced a great thing that day. He did not speak much because God was in control. He said, "You went right in and said, 'I am here to talk about Jesus.' You did not have to wait for an opening to speak about Him." I did not have the gift of mercy, but I did have the gift of exhortation, which is giving people hope. I could give her the hope of heaven. I could give her hope in Christ. She was not going to die, she was going to live forever with Jesus.

I started going to her home while she was on hospice. I would go and sing to her and read her my stories I wrote about the hope of heaven and Christ. I would tell her about heaven and the celebration there will be at her entrance. No one really knows the time of our death, but we know God is always in control. Sharon lived nine more months without chemo. She was left here long enough for her estranged stepchild to give her a Mother's Day card saying *I love you* for the first time, and she got to see her first grandbaby born. She was ready for heaven, and God was ready for her.

There were two ministers at her funeral. The first was an older man; he spoke of her and her life on earth. The second minister spoke of the celebration and how we should celebrate this great day as she enters the kingdom of God. I wore a bright colored turquoise blouse, just for Sharon, in celebration of her life on earth and on her entrance into God presence. I felt honored that God would choose me to comfort His child.

Obeying the call on my life was what I wanted to do most. God arranged it all, and my job was to go. I wanted to help others to know Christ. I wanted to serve the Lord; in this way I could live my life fully for the Lord.

2 TIMOTHY 3:16

"All scripture is inspired by God and is useful for
teaching the truth, rebuking error, correcting faults,
and giving instruction for right living."

Every word in the Bible is God breathed and is true. So when you
read the words in the Bible, read them knowing they were written
to you. Meditate closely on every word for it will have instruction
on how God wants you to live and bring Him glory. The Word of
God also has a lot to say about your faults and failings and how you
can be forgiven. God also corrects you when you are living outside
of His will for you. Pay attention to the correction, it is for your
good and God's glory.

And always remember, God is teaching you through His word.
Pray for the knowledge of God. The Bible says the truth will set
you free… free to be His.

GOD'S MINISTRY

Most people who know God know the Lord's Prayer, but do we live by God's word and God's will? It says God's will is to be done on earth. He knows what He wants us to do, but are we willing to do it here on earth? I am now a surrendered Christian. That means I have given up the control of my life for God to use me for His purpose. I pray, "Use me Lord," and He does just that. He not only uses me, he prepares me for the task, and He never fails me.

God began His preparation on me March 19, 1995, and I began His work on May 22, 1995. Nine weeks to prepare my heart and mind to begin my mission work for the Lord. My missionary work was in my own back yard. I had been in bed a lot during those weeks, but I felt it was part of His plan too. He prepared me by teaching me love, compassion, patience, and perseverance. He gave me power through His word and showed me the power of prayer.

When God puts things in our heart, the mission begins. Here is how it all came about. On March 6, I felt the urge to write to the pastor who told me about Jesus that day at Hanover church many years ago. I also sent him one of my writings about how without someone telling me about Jesus and His death on the cross for me, I would not be going to heaven. I thanked him and told him I would always remember him and how thankful I was that he told me the good news.

On March 19, my husband and I went to hear Lowel Lund-sturm the evangelist, for eight nights straight. The things he said stirred my heart. He said we should not be content just being Christians, but we should share the promise of Jesus with others. He said there would be choirs of people in heaven because we loved God enough to tell others about Him. He spoke of God's love for me, and my heart was renewed, and I longed to serve the Lord even more.

On April 7, I invited some of my friends to the Teen Challenge Banquet in our town. It was a fundraiser, and the evening was very nice. Men spoke of their addictions and how God and God alone changed their lives; someone told them how Jesus could save them by His death on the cross. One of my friends told me about his new ministry with the Gideons and how they were going to the county jail to have church for the men. He said there was a real need for a women's ministry there.

After speaking to my friend, I turned around and there was the student, who was the speaker, talking to my husband. In a room of five hundred people, he found us, and we talked for about twenty minutes about how he was going into the streets of Chicago to tell homeless people about Jesus. He was going to the very bad areas to share what he had learned about Jesus' death for our sins. I found a stirring in my heart. I had the longing to go to the jails and start a Bible study for the women.

I began to pray about this, I wanted God to be in control, so I prayed His will be done on earth. If I were the servant to carry this message to the jail, it would be by God's will. After weeks of prayer, I began calling to see how to get a women's ministry into the county jail. I called a friend who is a parole officer, he told me to go to the Ministerial Alliance and work through them. So I began calling ministers to get just the right man in just the right town to help. After ten ministers, I reached Rev. Rhodes, head of the Ministerial Alliance in Jackson, a neighboring town. He was also one of the ministers who gave the devotion at the evangelistic crusade I attended in March. He said he would work on it for me.

I put this ministry on prayer lists throughout our community. Then I was to have patience, for God was at work in me. Then on April 19, the Oklahoma bombing happened. My heart was touched as I watched people, on the TV news, love and helps one another. I was being lifted up and saw God's compassion for all people and how He wanted me to have this kind of compassion.

During this time, I led three Bible studies a week. I learned about obeying God when He calls you. In Genesis with Abraham, Isaac and Jacob, I learned how God calls each of us for His purpose. In James, I learned about prayer and its power. On May 5, my disease got worse, and I learned a lesson about perseverance. Out of twenty-one days in May, I was in bed ten of those days. I never missed a Bible study because sharing God's word was so important, it did not matter how I felt, so I would get up and go to the study for an hour and then back to bed.

Rev. Rhodes finally called, and I got in jail the hard way. I was to go to jail every Monday night at 7:00 p.m. I called the Stonecroft Ministries to see if they would supply me with Bibles. I was thankful God had answered my prayers and put me in jail.

When Tuesday night rolled around, I was flat on my back at 6:30 p.m. Satan was working hard on me; I had a headache all afternoon. I got up and went to the car and drove to the neighboring town to lead the Bible Study for the women in the county jail. God was faithful and when I got to jail I felt better. I put my trust in the Lord.

I was in the waiting room when the Gideons arrived, and one of them said he had been praying for a women's ministry in jail for two years. As we got into the elevator, he asked if he could pray for the women and me. We held hands and prayed all the way to the basement on the elevator. When the door opened, the matron led me to the lunchroom. It had a broken TV set, some paperback books leaning against the wall, and a picnic table in the center of the room; that was all. I asked the Matron how many girls were in jail, and she said eight.

They came out one-by-one. One then two, praise God, three, four, five, thank you Lord, six, seven, and then eight. One hundred percent all the praise and glory go to the Lord for all He has done. Now the evening was His, and I would be the vessel He would use. The mission had begun. God stirred my heart and equipped me for His good work here on earth. God calls us and equips us to do his work, and I was called and equipped in 1995.

God called me to jail. Some are sent to jail by judges, but I was called to go. I never wanted to be in jail. God put me there, and I must always remember this is His ministry, not mine. I am truly not adequate enough to minister to the ladies I met each week, but God is. I truly believe God called me to this ministry and equipped me. It is a calling on my life and every week I longed to give up one night to go to jail for God.

The main preparation I did each week was prayer. All week I prayed for the girls. All day on Tuesday I prayed for them. I prayed all the way to Jackson. Then I'd sit in front of the jail and pray, "Empty me of myself and fill me with you, Lord. You know these ladies in this place, and you know what they need, so I trust you and you alone." Then I would go in and just trust God.

When I introduced myself, every night I said "Hello, I'm Pat the Avon Lady." I'd get a laugh and their trust. After all I was an Avon lady for over 30 years. They want someone who can help them with their fear. They wanted someone who could show them a way to have peace. I would always tell the girls in jail that I prayed to get in, and they'd say they were praying to get out. Every Tuesday evening was different, because the ladies were different, and I didn't know what exactly would happen on Tuesday evening. I never knew how many ladies would come to the Bible study. I didn't have to know because God knew, and I trusted Him. Sometimes I'd play music and sometimes I'd read a devotion to begin the evening. We read the word of God, meditated, and studied it. Sometimes we did a formal Bible study. Some nights I thought I knew what would happen, and then I would do something completely different after I got there because the Spirit of God directed it.

I would see the same girls over and over, year after year. I was never discouraged because they returned again and again. When I sin repeatedly, Jesus is never discouraged with me. Jesus waits for me to listen to Him. So I would do the same with the ladies in jail. I just kept speaking the word of God, over and over, like Jesus did.

God has given me such love for these strangers. As I looked into their eyes, all I saw was the child God wanted for His own. So I prayed for them to know Him better. All they needed was Jesus in their lives. They needed to surrender to God's will. I won't know if God's word took root in their hearts until I get to heaven. But I pray it did.

God gave me such compassion and love for the ladies in jail. I wanted to be with them and give them comfort and a hope for a future that would not harm them. I wanted their days to be filled with the peace and joy we receive from God. I would tell the girls in jail that one day they would thank God for the time they spent in jail, in His presence. When God changes our lives and we are renewed, we are always thankful. I wanted them to remember when they cried out for Him, and He was there.

Many girls came to know Jesus as their Savior while in jail. I remember Jennifer, one of the inmates, who surrendered her will to God's will and quit running from Him. She was sentenced to four months in prison, instead she asked the judge for two years at Teen Challenge. She wanted to walk closer to the Lord when she got out. She wanted to get stronger in the Lord, knowing that His strength would keep her life free of drugs. She wanted the peace that passes all understanding the Bible speaks about, that only God can give.

She wanted to be a new creation in Christ. Jennifer is married to a minister.

I gave eight Bibles to ladies who had never seen a Bible. I gave Lori her first Bible; she wondered why the first four books of the New Testament kept repeating themselves. Once, I gave a Bible to two eighteen-year-old girls who stole a car in our town. They were from Kansas City, Missouri. They stayed up all night reading God's Word. When they wrote home to their boyfriends, they told them, "Get this wonderful book they call the Bible. It is awesome."

It was hard for me to realize that someone could live in the heartland and never have seen a Bible. I asked one young girl why she had never seen a Bible before. She said her mom never took her to church. She said, "At the age of eleven, I was getting high on drugs with my mother." One day in jail, there were two girls who came to know Jesus the Savior of the world for the first time. When they went back to their cells and the matron unlocked the door to let us out of the day room, she noticed the girls were changed. She said, "You look different. What happened in there?" She could see God's presence in their faces.

I thank God He put me in jail, just to be in His presence for two hours a week. Just to see Him change lives. This is the best thing that happened to me every week for fourteen years. To see God's promises come true. He can make us new creations if we are in Christ Jesus. We are truly saved by grace, and He said we would have a renewing of our minds. When I left jail to go home each week, I would say, "Thank you, Jesus, thank you, Jesus, thank you, Jesus."

ROMANS 3:16

"Ruin and misery mark their ways."

This verse speaks of the unrighteous Romans. The Bible says there is none righteous, not even one. Pain and agony filled the earth. Suffering and sin was the way of life for the people there. No matter how hard they tried to be righteous, they failed.

It is the same way now. No matter how good we are, we will never meet the standard God has set before us. We could never be righteous on our own. God sees our unworthiness. God wants all to be saved and we cannot do it on our own. God didn't want ruin and misery to mark our ways all the rest of our lives. That is why He sent His Son, Jesus, to save us. Jesus died to free us from misery and ruin. Jesus made us righteous in God is sight. Jesus did it for me and for you so we could live upright and holy lives. Through faith in Jesus Christ we are saved.

JAIL

The beginning of the jail ministry was a blessing for me. It taught me so much, but most of all I walked closer to God than ever before. Each week I spent time in the Word, in God's presence, trusting Him to give me the words I needed. The night evolved as God willed it. I surrendered it all to God and let Him have control. I let the Holy Spirit that dwelled within me lead my every word.

The ladies had a hunger and thirst for the word of God. When I asked them to read God's word, they were as excited as if I had told them to look for a hundred dollar bill among the pages of the Bible. Coming to the Bible Study was their choice, so I counted it a privilege to meet them. The ladies came from all kinds of church backgrounds: Baptist, Methodist, Pentecost, and Non-Denominational. There were Jews, Muslims, and Satin worshippers; some had never been in a church in their lives.

The second time I went to jail, the presence of God went before me for I prayed all day and trusted God totally. The first week they came in one-by-one, but this week they were waiting on me; they had done their homework and wanted more of the Word. When I looked into their eyes, all I could see were children of God. My love for them was overwhelming. I could love these strangers more than anyone on earth. I did not see prisoners, inmates, convicts, or bad girls, I saw ladies that God wanted to be His.

One cold night in January of 1996, I had a night to remember. These girls were on my mind all week. Each time I thought of them, I'd pray for them. When I went in, I said, "I'm here to do the women's Bible study." The clerk responded, "Go right down, the matron will meet you at the door." I went to the elevator with my tape player in one hand and a big bag of Bibles in the other. The matron met me as promised and said, "We are really glad you could be here tonight. The girls really need you. We have had a bad week, and about half the girls are on suicide watch." The matron then locked me in the day room and went to get the girls.

I waited, and when the door was opened again, in came all eight girls. Four sat at the table ready to study God's Word. The other four went to the farthest corner and sat on the floor. One of the girls was very angry. She said to me, "I want to see the sheriff. This is against my rights. If I want to go to church or not, I had the right to choose." When the girls were on suicide watch they have to stay together and not be alone. I told her to just ignore me, I wouldn't mind. She began to write something and wouldn't look up. She had dark hair and big dark eyes but didn't give her name. She mumbled to the blonde girl next to her, "Jail is not the place to start going back to church, it's too late now." The blonde was reading a book and really never looked up all evening.

The other two girls on the floor had come to Bible study a lot during their stay, but tonight they were angry and upset. Patty had tried to commit suicide last week and was sent to the state mental hospital for observation; now she was back and not talking to me. Pam was supposed to be released last week after five months, but with red tape she was still in jail. She was upset, very upset. "I can't stay here anymore," she said. "I'm nervous, and I just feel like walking. I am angry and I can't do this anymore. I am not crazy I just can't stand this. I'm not crazy." I could feel the unrest, like there were four time bombs ready to go off over in the corner. Alice was at the table; she was on the suicide watch since last week too. Every week since she had been arrested, Alice cried about her brother who was murdered. We could not sing "Amazing Grace" because it would upset her too much.

I prayed for the Holy Spirit to take over and fill the room with peace. I began to play music; the first song was moving. The lesson that evening was on the elements of prayer. We talked about intercessory prayer. Jesus is our intercessor; He goes to the Father for us so we can be free of sin. We read a lot of verses from the word of God it guided the evening.

> In the same way, the Spirit helps us in our weakness. We do not know what we ought to pray for, but the Spirit himself intercedes for us with groans that words cannot express. And he who searches our hearts knows the mind of the Spirit.
>
> Romans 8:26–27

> They should always pray and not give up.
>
> Luke 18:1

> Pray continually.
>
> 1 Thessalonians 5:17

The girls marked these verses; they knew they needed God's presence in their lives. We talked about praying for each other.

There was a new girl at the table; she was very, very quiet. She never spoke or read; she was just lost in her thoughts. We read another verse from the bible,

> And pray in the Spirit on all occasions with all kinds of prayers and requests. With this in mind, be alert and always keep on praying for all the saints.
>
> Ephesians 6:18

The girls at the table were encouraged, but as we talked and as we read, Patty, on the floor, wept. Pam hugged her and wept with her. The dark haired, dark eyed girl stopped writing and was listening. The blonde kept reading. When the lesson was over I closed in prayer for the girls. Then I played them another song. This song touched their hearts too; music always stirred their heart. As the music played, they began to change. When the song ended the whole group was quiet. God touched lives that night, and I was there as a witness and they would never be the same.

Alice asked me if we could sing "Amazing Grace" after all these months. She led the song with a twinkle in her eye, not a tear. The dark haired, dark eyed girl stood up and sang out after being so angry. She wanted to sing more and lead us in more songs about Jesus. The darkness had lifted, and you could feel God's presence. During the singing, Patty came over to me and said she was sorry she wasn't there last week but would be back next week. Pam was smiling and clapping and singing.

The blonde girl on the floor was still reading her romance novel; she never looked up. Maybe she never heard about God that night, maybe she doesn't know Him. But God will send someone else to tell her again. Just before I left for the night, the quiet new girl came to me, touched my hand, and said, "Pray for me."

Another girl who broke my heart when I met her was Rochelle. She had blonde hair with black roots, black eyebrows, and baby blue eyes. There were big tears in her eyes when we met. The matron warned me before I went in that there were two new girls who would cause trouble. I introduced myself as the Avon Lady, and I was there to tell them about Jesus. Rochelle never went to church before. She was quiet and did not speak but listened, and the tears that were in her eyes welled up and began to stream down her face. I told her of God's love for her, and she never took her eyes off me. Rochelle wept and began sucking her thumb; she was seventeen years old and a baby at heart. She never spoke the first night; she just cried.

The next week, Rochelle's eyes were bright, and she told me she always believed there was a God but didn't really know this Jesus. She began to tell her story of a life that was stolen by the world: a story of a seventeen-year-old that never began living. She said she was always a bad girl. Her mother gave her over to the state at the age of three years old. For years she was in and out of foster care, then juvenile detention centers, and now she was turned over to the county to keep. She had years of drug abuse. Her father turned her on to drugs for the first time at eleven when she stayed with him a short time when he wasn't in prison. She overdosed once causing her to be unconscious for three days. She had scars on her arms from self-inflicted cuts and cigarette burns. She had scars on her wrists from suicide attempts. She wanted to inflict pain on herself, as if she didn't have enough already. She also thought she was pregnant.

We talked about Jesus' love and how she was precious to Him. Rochelle's mother was a drug addict, and her father a prisoner, and now Rochelle was both. All I wanted was for her to know, for sure, that God loved her, and He would give her the peace and joy that she did not have. Since her birth, she was an unwanted, uneducated child of the streets. That night in jail, this lost person learned that she had a heavenly Father. She learned Jesus loved her and that she was precious to Him. She learned she was a child of God and that He would never leave her nor forsake her. She learned that God never makes a mistake. She was put on the earth for a purpose, and even if her parents didn't want her, God did.

In 1997, I met a girl named April. She didn't speak much the first night, but her eyes were filled with tears most of the time. When the study was over, she asked for my address so she could write me during the week. She wrote and told me how depressed she was and said she remembered what she learned as a child about

Jesus. She said she grew up in church and always loved God. Her home was seventy miles away, and she was lonely. She dearly loved her twin brothers, but now was estranged from her family because of jail. She wrote about getting her life right and how her mom wouldn't accept her telephone calls anymore. She said she had no earthly being to turn to, now that her family turned their backs on her. She was there to learn how to have a relationship with Jesus

The next week she was there with her baby blue. I was the only person in Cape she knew that went to church, and she asked to go to church with me when she got out. She was a smart girl and went to college in our town, majoring in music at the university, after being married to an abusive husband for a few years. With poor self-esteem and longing for friends in her college town, she befriended the wrong people. This all led her to a criminal life of forgery; she was alone and scared.

She served her time in the county jail and paid for her crimes, and she was released in October after ninety days in jail. I was visiting a friend's mother-in-law; she was an eighty-one-year-old Hungarian woman who hadn't been to church in years. My friend asked me to tell her mother-in-law about Jesus. After that visit, I arrived home at 4:00 p.m. after being gone all day, and there was April sitting on my front porch. She had been there since 9:00 a.m., having walked from Jackson, eight miles away. She had big tears in her baby blue eyes that just cried out, "Help me." She was homeless, penniless, hungry, and only had the summer clothes on her back. I invited her in and as I fixed dinner, April cried. That night she went to choir practice with me. I didn't know what plans God had for April, but we trusted God. She joined the choir that night, and she was back in church.

April was going to spend the night with me, and before bed she came over and gave me a hug and a kiss and said, "Thank you." I couldn't fall asleep that night. I tossed and turned. I worried about my stuff. I didn't trust April. She was convicted of stealing checks and forging them. My human nature seemed to get the best of me. As the quietness of the night passed, I prayed. At 3:00 a.m., a peace came over me; I knew what I was to do. I was to trust God; I didn't need to trust April. I fell asleep and never again felt fear from April; she was God's child too.

The next morning, the adventure began. We got in the car, and I prayed for the day. I asked for God to direct us. In the next six days we saw God's provision. He provided clothes, two jobs, job uniforms, daily needs, plenty of food, and the money needed to rent her apartment.

After a few years, April left town, and I did not hear from her until four years later. I got a call from her. She was homeless once more. This time her second husband got a court order to keep her out of the house and away from her two small daughters. She was in a motel and needed help. He had the police take her car from her while she was at work. This all happened two days before Christmas. I helped to get her into the Safe House for Women and helped her get to court. She got her two small daughters back. God was watching after her once more. We went to get her clothes with a police escort, and her second abusive husband had thrown her clothes into the snow in the front yard. We gathered her belongings, and she began a new life once more because God was watching over April.

The experiences I had in jail are too numerous to tell about, but one of the girls that stands out in my mind is Kacy. She was the biggest drug dealer in New Madrid County. She came to know Christ as her Savior in the Cape county jail. She was an inspiration to the girls in jail and went on to prison where she touched many lives for Christ. She graduated from sixty correspondent Bible studies while she was in the county for over a year with me.

Kacy's testimony relates that when she was selling drugs, she had everything she ever wanted: money, cars, and clothes; in the County Jail she wore an orange jump suit and orange rubber shoes.

She drank out of her peanut butter jar and slept on a mat on the floor, but she was happier than she had ever been in her entire life because she had Jesus in her life. I also remember Ferrell, who did not know Christ at all. The first night in jail, she came into a relationship with the Lord that was strong. She was not afraid to go to prison because she was not alone. She thanked God for sending her to jail too, because it saved her life.

Broken lives now renewed because God gave up His Son for them. I could see the change in their eyes. There were girls who wrote poetry and others who drew wonderful pictures because of their new life in Christ. They would sing and praise God. When I was gone during the week, they would have their own Bible studies and devotion time. They would minister to one another. God was with them all the time. When new girls would come in with the world all over them, there would be turmoil until they too came to know Christ. Some of the girls read the Bible five times while in the county jail. They spent their time growing in Christ.

I was blessed every night I went to jail. I am so thankful God sent me there. I grew in my faith and knowledge of Christ too. I obeyed my calling and followed my Spirit into jail. It is through that obedience that our lives are fuller. When we live life fully we would be in places we never wanted to go but were sent, we would be out of our comfort zone and in the presence of God.

1 JOHN 3:16

"This is how we know what love is: Christ gave his life for us. We too, then, ought to give our lives for our brothers!"

Every day of our lives as Christians, we should become a little more like Jesus. The more we get to know Him, the more like Him we should be. Jesus loved us so much that He gave it all. He did not think about His life, He thought about yours and mine. He put us first. That is what love is, putting others first, above our own desires. Sacrificing for others. Do we? This is hard for us in a self-centered world. But if we put Christ first with in our lives and become Christ-centered then we could love like Jesus and give up our lives for our brothers. We should put others first, love the unlovely, share the gospel, and really care about other people and their lives.

HELPING OTHERS

There were many opportunities to serve the Lord through counseling others and Bible studies, and I began to wonder if I needed training in the area of counseling. I prayed to give all the people I counseled the true word of God and not my words. I prayed for His guidance.

In a few weeks, a letter from Liberty University came for me. It was a Baptist Bible College. I got a scholarship to take the correspondence courses. I signed up and majored in Christian counseling. All of the courses were on tape, and I needed a proctor to grade the tests. I asked my son Tim to be the proctor, so I began. I learned a lot. I took other courses in evangelism, teaching Sunday school, all the books of the Bible, and many other courses. It really helped me to grow in my Christian faith. I never finished because I did not take the finals or finish the doctrine part of the Baptist College because I was Lutheran, but I feel I learned enough to council others.

I counseled a lot of friends with trouble in their lives. I remember an older friend who was getting a divorce after thirty-five years of marriage; her husband was having an affair with one of her friends. She would come to my house in the wee hours of the night, crying, and I would sit and talk to her for hours about God's love for her. I told her she could come or call any hour, night or day, and she did. Another friend called me to come over. I did and found out her husband had left her for another woman; she was devastated. The woman was her former secretary and now was her husband's secretary and lover. There was a bitter divorce and lots of anger. I pointed her to Jesus, who can heal all anger and pain. Both women found a new life after the divorce with Christ at the center.

My son, Scott, had a friend that was leaving for service but did not want to leave his widowed mother by herself and asked me to watch after her. For five years we were constant friends, and I took the place of her son till he returned. We would call on the phone and talk for hours a day. I talked about God's love and kept reminding her of God's promises to her as she clung to me during the time her son was gone. When her son returned, she was fine once more.

An Avon customer asked me to sit with her husband while she had a mastectomy. I had never met her husband. We sat all day talking together. After the surgery, I helped her at her home. We became close friends. She was twenty years older than me, and was a very colorful friendly person.

I had another friend who was twenty years younger than me, and she wasn't even married when we met. She got married and had fertility problems, but later had four children. Before the first child was born, she was terrified of going to the hospital. She was confused about a lot of things, and we began a Bible study together.

One day, we read the book of Colossians together. I talked about the Good News of Jesus, and she didn't know what I was talking about. I told her, and she said she had never heard of it before, yet she went to church every Sunday. I told her to listen to her priest, and she would hear about Jesus and His death just for her.

The next week, she said she heard the priest talk about Jesus and His death and resurrection for her. She sat there every week and never heard the message, but when it was time, God opened her eyes. She marked in her Bible the day we read Colossians as the day she was saved.

She was afraid of the hospital, but with Jesus by her side she was no longer afraid. We talked about parenting and being a wife; I became her mentor. I shared my experiences with her as a wife and mother. We were so alike because she thought like I did about home making, cooking, and kids. She was more like me than anyone I had ever known. She raised four wonderful children and was a great homemaker and wife.

I came to know Mary. She went to church with me, and when I was superintendent of the Sunday schools at our church, Mary was a teacher. After a teacher's meeting, Mary was weeping. I gave her a hug and asked her if she would like to come to my home every Wednesday on her lunch hour for a Bible study. She agreed, and that's when our friendship began. I was her mentor, and we talked about God and His plan for our lives. She spoke of the pain in her life and of losing her son to SID's. As she grew in Christ, our friendship grew too. We were good friends who loved the Lord. I got to see her mature in Christ, and eventually, I invited her to jail with me. She still comes for lunch, and we talk about Jesus. We agree that we are spiritual friends and always talk about Jesus and the Bible when we are together.

Each of us has a comfort zone, and sometimes God calls us out of it and stirs our hearts till we can do nothing else but obey the calling. Once, a friend talked about her son-in-law who was in bed with a backache. He had been in bed for weeks. She wanted the pastor to call on him, but he had not been there yet. I felt like going by to see Mike. He was thirty-three years old and could hardly get out of bed. I took devotions and songs along; I read and sang to him. We talked about Jesus and his eyes lit up. I went back every week.

Later he was diagnosed with cancer and became very ill with chemo and still not able to get out of bed. He knew Jesus as his Savior and went to heaven to be with Him.

God makes you bold in faith, and He gives you the courage to get out of that comfort zone. After Mike's death, my spirit urged me to teach a Bible study at the local homeless shelter. I was out of my comfort zone there too, but God always equips us. I went there for weeks because I felt that it would honor Mike's life if I gave up some of mine for others. I did not send flowers to Mike's funeral, I told others about Jesus because of him.

One night, there was a big black man who had been in prison for gang related activities living at the shelter; he came to my Bible study. While I spoke, he paced in the back of the room. He had been rude to the owner before class and seemed very nervous. As the class went on he did sit down and became less restless. When the class ended, he hit his hand on the table very hard and said, "Now that was a good Bible study," then he stood up and left the room. God's presence was there, and I spoke the words that man needed that night because of God. I never saw him again.

I met a couple at the homeless shelter that stayed there for a while. She was raised next door to my parents, and I knew her since she was a little girl. I remember when she came to swim at my mom's pool and was afraid to get into the water because the deep water might come over to the shallow end, and she wanted to know what kept that water over on the deep side. This couple was living in sin and this was a Christian homeless shelter so they were married in the sight of God to be able to live in the shelter together. They were truck drivers and had a lot of trouble with drugs on the road. They had lost their five children to the state, and they were living with their grandparents. Now the couple was staying in this homeless shelter and trying to straighten out their lives.

They attended the class every night I was there for months, then one day they were no longer there. They had left the homeless shelter, started using drugs again, and were living in their car. One night, they came to my home at two o'clock in the morning and were banging on my doors and windows and yelling. I did not let them in because they were high on drugs.

The next day, they called and wanted to come by, and I told them they could. We sat in the garage at a table and chairs I had set up. I knew they wanted money; I did give them a little money, but first I talked about Jesus and his love for them for two hours. They left, and the next time I heard from them was about two years later. They cleaned up their lives and were better. They had jobs, a home, and their 5 children back, and they wanted me to know how Jesus was the center of their lives now. They had lived in the basement of a church for months, and the minister there mentored them in their new walk with the Lord.

Three years passed, and the lady rang my doorbell one Saturday afternoon. She said I was on her mind, Jesus was her Lord and the Holy Spirit was her guide. So as her spirit led, she stopped by to see me. She wanted to thank me for introducing her to Jesus. I really didn't understand what she was talking about. She said, "The first time I ever heard about Jesus was when you took me to Vacation Bible School when I was a little girl, and now he is my Savior and Lord. I just want to thank you."

That's how it works. God planted the seed at Vacation Bible School, then He watered it throughout her life at the homeless shelter and other places, and when it took root and began to grow, there was a harvest. God could have arranged for someone else to plant the seed, but he chose me.

We never know when God is at work in people's hearts, so we should always act upon the call. I had the compassion only God gives, and I would sing to my ill friends and read them the stories that I would write. I felt they received comfort from the music. The background tapes I had were songs I sang when I was very ill with my muscles; the songs spoke of pain and God's presence through it. I would write from an ill person's point of view about how I needed to trust God with all things. The songs and stories would point to God.

Three of us started a Bible study for ladies with troubles in their lives, and we would have luncheons and hear God's word. I invited my friend Ruth. She found out she had cancer right after her retirement and it was very bad. I took her to this Bible study so she would have strength to endure her coming months. I would go by her house on her bad days and sing to her and read the stories about Jesus that I wrote.

Ruth was a warrior during her four-year bout with cancer, and she won because she went to heaven with dignity and in peace, knowing Jesus loved her. I also sang to Margaret after her hip replacement went bad. She got a blood disease that put her into bed for months, and she went without a hip for a year. She would light up when I would come over to talk to her and sing. She still talks about our time together.

God sent me to various places to do Bible studies, and I was always willing to go. I went to senior centers to teach studies with the elderly. I taught at the safe house that was for battered and abused women, and I had a study at the Vision house, which is a home for recovering addicts. I went wherever God wanted me to be.

I counseled women at Birthright, a pregnancy crisis center, for five years. I talked about Jesus to the girls there, and they came to know Jesus. I would get them into a Christian unwed mothers' home and they could learn more about Jesus and have their babies. Some would give them up for adoption and some would keep them, but no one would abort them. I would give out clothes to needy mothers with small children; I would give out food and formula.

I also worked on the fish hot line, which gave food out to the needy from the local food pantry. I never met the people but had the opportunity to speak to them about God and His love. God wants us to help the helpless, and I wanted to do that for Him. We can never do enough for the needy and helpless. But when we are urged by the spirit inside of us to help, we should act on the calling that is how we live life fully for the Lord.

1 PETER 3:16

"But do it with gentleness and respect. Keep your conscience clear; so that when you are insulted, those who speak evil of your good conduct as followers of Christ will become ashamed of what they say."

The sentence before this verse says," *be ready at all times to answer anyone who asks you to explain the hope you have in you.*" People who don't know Jesus, as Lord and Savior, sometimes want to cause Christians harm, by saying hurtful things to them and about them. They want to make us angry so we act ungodly.

Beware! Keep your guard up against the evil foe! The word of God has good instruction on how we should act when this happens to us. First, we are to be ready to tell them of our hope in Christ with gentleness and respect. Then, do not act like the world acts, keep your conscience clear and do right. Always stand firm in your faith and keep acting like followers of Christ. Finally, remember they are not rejecting you but Jesus.

LIFE'S LESSONS

I wrote a lot about life and the lessons we learn through living. One day someone said to me, "I can't believe you said that." It really set me to thinking about being an example to others who watch me. Maybe they do not know the Lord. Maybe they need a lighthouse to go to, and would I be that lighthouse for others to see in the dark, or would I discourage them by my bad example. I needed to keep my eyes on Jesus and act like a child of God all the time. The next writings are about being examples and following the Lord.

Stranger Here

> To this you were called, because Christ suffered for you, leaving you an example that you should follow in His steps.
>
> 1 Peter 2:21

Jesus set a great example for us. We long to have the character of Jesus; we want to be like Him. The Bible speaks of us being like Jesus. Every day that we walk in the Lord, we become more like Him. The more we read the word of God, the more we learn about Jesus who was a great example for us. This was God's plan for us to grow in spirit and knowledge of the one true God.

We wear the popular WWJD (What Would Jesus Do) bracelets symbolizing our desire to follow God's leadership. We consider our behavior and ask ourselves: What would the Son of God do? So we model ourselves after Jesus, the Son of Man. If we are to become like Him and do all He did, shouldn't we expect suffering in our lives as well? Shouldn't we expect people to ridicule us because of our faith? Shouldn't they hate us? If we feel like strangers here, then we are moving in the right direction. We are moving closer to Christ. Every day we should become more like Christ in every way, even in our suffering for His sake.

Are we really martyrs for Christ? Do we boldly step forward and uphold the Word of God, telling everyone His Word is the truth? Do we tell others about Jesus, the Savior of the world, who died for all mankind? Or, are we afraid of offending others with our bold faith? What will they think of us? What will they say about us? They may say we are radical Christians or call us Jesus freaks. All I can say is, if we are called names because of our faith, hallelujah and praise the Lord they noticed we are children of God! They noticed that we are strangers here.

He suffered more ridicule then we will ever suffer. Jesus did it all for us. What little discomfort we encounter is very minor compared to what He had to endure. 1 Peter also tells us that Jesus left us an example that we should follow in the steps of Jesus. That means we are to walk His walk, act the way He acts, and love the way He loves. We need to carry His cross and boldly speak up for Jesus. He already did it all for us, He gained our victory over sin and death and set us free to live forever. All we must do is tell others of our wonderful Savior, Jesus. We must walk into His marvelous light, so we will feel like strangers here.

The Master's Feet

My greatest wish is to sit at your feet and learn from you. I long to be with you all the time, and I seek your presence in my life. Yet, I have many things that distract me and keep me from you. Things of this world stand between us and keep me preoccupied. I long to be with you at every moment of every day. Why am I so full of the world and not You, God?

This is the prayer of a person who wants to be a Mary and not a Martha in her spiritual life, like the Bible speaks of in Luke 10:38. She has volunteered to do all that is offered in service to the Lord. She worked hard to give all she could give, expecting nothing in return. She did everything for God, doing it as well as she could, wanting to be excellent for Him. She didn't care what others thought, she didn't do it for them; she did it for the Lord. It was always for Him because she loved Jesus and longed to be with Him. Her heart was good, and her eyes were on the Lord; yet, she felt empty and unfulfilled. There was a stirring in her heart to know the Savior more. She wanted to be taught by the Master and walk in His ways, not in hers. How could this be done?

> But seek first His kingdom and His righteousness, and all these things will be given to you as well.
>
> Matthew 6:33

All the directions are in the Holy book: The Bible. Now, if she would just go to the Word, she would find God.

The Bible says,

> Ask and it will be given to you; seek and you will find; knock and the door will be opened to you. For everyone who asks receives; he who seeks finds and to him who knocks, the door will be opened.
>
> Matthew 7:7–8

She must do as the Word of God directs because Christ is her strength.

Let us thank God in advance for the power she is about to receive in Jesus' name. She is about to go on a spiritual journey, in the presence of God. He will show her the way and lead her closer to Him. He will teach her His ways, give her His heart and His mind. She will be at His feet as He prepares her to be used by Him!

She should pray, telling God who He is to her and should thank God for all He has done and will do for her. She should acknowledge the power of God in her life and remember God has a plan for everyone on this earth, that plan is to know Him. Not all will come to know Him and not all who know him will live for Him the way He wants them to. We never know all God has planned, that is why we must read the Bible; the Bible will direct us, which leads us closer to Him.

Sometimes our lives are not full of the Lord's joy. Yet, that is what God wants for every one of his children: to be so full of God we are overflowing with joy! To have so much peace of the Lord in our lives that in the midst of turmoil, we are peaceful inside. We know God is in control, He can sanctify us and make us holy, if we allow Him. We must long to be Christ-centered, and not self-centered. We should be at his feet, seeking to know Him better every day. We should surrender our will to His will and live for Him, not for ourselves.

God sent His only son to die for us. He wants us to be totally committed to being in His presence with Him as our Lord and Master. The way is not an easy way because of the old nature in us, but His way is the only way, then we will have peace and joy. God can help if you pray and ask Him to help. When you live the life God truly desires, you will not worry and want, you will be content and living for the Lord! Your life will be joyful and peaceful; you will be living for the Lord! The way you take will be easy, for you will be taking the way of the Lord. This is the best way for you to live. Learn from the Master and sit at His feet.

Privilege and Power

Jesus died. Yes, Jesus died for all mankind. God sent His son to earth for all to be saved and come to the knowledge of truth. There is nothing like the cross to show us the love of God. We can barely comprehend a love like this, so honest, so pure. Jesus wore a crown of thorns to forgive our sins; in exchange we receive His crown of glory. Eternal life becomes ours; we may now live forever with Him in glory.

It's time to go public for Jesus. It's time to move into action. What wonderful words Jesus spoke from the cross,

> Father, Forgive them, for they do not know what they are doing.
> Luke 23:34

He spoke these words for us, to allow freedom from our sins and freedom from temptation. We gain a new life when we know Jesus as our Savior.

Why do we lay dormant? With news like this we should not be able to keep silent. Yet we wait in silence, not speaking of the Christ who changed our lives, nor sharing the news with others. We were saved to serve God and bring Him glory. We need to be excited Jesus saves! We need to tell everyone, Jesus saves! Don't let anyone live life knowing you and not knowing Jesus.

You and I could never say enough about Jesus; we could never serve Him enough or love Him enough to equal His death on the cross for us. We could never sacrifice enough because there is no such thing as sacrificing too much for Jesus. Our commission is the same as Jesus' commission. He came to save all people. We need to tell all people about Jesus' death and resurrection, so God can save them. We have the privilege and power to do this.

When I think about Holy Week and Easter, I think of how great God truly is and how He loves all people. Jesus hung on that cross for me and for you. Our God is so great! He raised Jesus from the dead on Easter morning. God did this for us to have forgiveness and a new life in Christ. Now we can live eternally in heaven with Him forever. Strive to live your life so people can know Jesus Christ the Savior through you. Live your life in victory over sin and live a life of privilege and power.

First Place

> But seek first His kingdom and His righteousness, and all these things will be given to you as well.
>
> Matthew 6:33

When asked if God has first place in our lives, we readily echo, "Yes, oh yes! God has first place in my life. He is number one in my life, I love Him the most." Or just like Peter in the Bible, we say we will not deny Him, yet we do.

When Sunday comes, a day normally set aside to worship, we go to the soccer fields with our kids and skip church. We make no effort to go to the other services on other days; we just skip church. Instead, we choose our kids and their activity first. When we get the soccer schedule, we write the games on the calendar or hang the schedule on the refrigerator. We have no concern that there are six games on Sunday morning during church time. We would never consider skipping a game.

We believe our son or daughter is the key player of the game, and we are sure the game may be lost without our child. They could come in first place for the season and be real winners. Our child could be the star of the team. We choose the soccer game over worshiping God.

Or maybe we just had a hard week with lots of activities, and work was grueling. Our only day off is Sunday, a day of rest, according to the Bible. So we stay in bed and sleep late. We really want to be rested for the game on TV later. To make our life better, we miss church. Maybe we have an expensive boat, and Sunday is the only day we can go to the lake to rest and relax in the sun. We are in the presence of God when we enjoy His creation, so we know God is there; we rationalize and miss church.

We have a lack of commitment to God and do not keep Him first in our lives. We love Him, but we have our plans and they don't include Him. He has His place in our lives, and it is not first place.

What does God think of us when we do not choose Him first? He must be sad when He sees us sleeping, instead of worshipping. What a disappointment when we make excuses for not worshipping. He did not plan for our children His gifts from above to take first place in our hearts He wanted that position. He made the beauty of nature for us to enjoy, but not to replace Him.

God wants us to worship Him. God wants us to seek Him first and know Him better each day. God wants us to sing praises to Him and come unto Him. He made the angels in heaven to praise and worship Him, and He made us to praise him too because God loves our worship.

God wants us to come willingly to worship and have fellowship with other Christians. He wants us to have the best, and that is God. We need to live being good examples for our children, always keeping God in first place. Live your life in a way so that all who meet you know God is your first love. Live knowing there is nothing in this world that deserves first place in your life more than God.

Sheep

God's true sheep follow Him. They do the Father's will and seek the presence of God in their lives. Sheep are animals that follow, not lead. They have a master or shepherd to led them and guide them in every direction they may go. If they would be led to a cliff, and the first one would jump, all the sheep, one-by-one, would jump without hesitation. That is how God wants us to follow Him, without hesitation. He will not lead us into harm, but He will lead us into His the presence one day.

Jesus knows and cares for His sheep. We, the people of God, need to be trusting God in all situations. We need to, as the Bible says,

> Trust in the Lord with all of your heart, and lean not on your own understanding; in all your ways acknowledge Him, and He will makeyour paths straight.
>
> Proverbs 3:5-6

Christians claim Christ, yet lean on their own understanding, not His. We want God to fit into our self-made life, and we question God when the way He guides us becomes difficult or takes away from our life's pleasures.

We need to trust God without hesitation, and we need to trust enough to loosen the grip that we have on things of this world. It would be very hard for us to get enough strength from ourselves to release the grip we have on the world and all that is in it, but we don't have to do that. All we have to do is trust in the Lord with all our heart. You and I can all be true sheep if we allow God to direct our paths. To some, this is an almost impossible task because of our strong willfulness. We need to pray for guidance and belief.

God is so Almighty that He came to change his people. Even you and I can be transformed into children of the light. We should be dramatically changed to look and love more like Jesus. We should be willing to come out of our comfort zone and live and love for Christ.

Call upon the Lord in every situation, and let Him live in you and through you. Let the plan God already has for you determine your day!

God's Children

God is an Almighty God. I always knew this, but yesterday I had a new thought. God has no grandchildren. All of His children come to Him by the power of the Holy Spirit, one-on-one. Parents cannot bring them, others cannot save them, and they come on their own because Jesus is their Savior.

As much as we want our children to be saved, we cannot save them. All we can do is love the Lord so much that He shows through our lives, to be examples. Even though they are our children, they do not automatically become God's grandchildren. We need to understand our part in this. We are to love them, nurture them, care for them, and tell them of God's love for them. We are to speak of Jesus to our children and pray for them every day. God is our Heavenly Father, and we are His children and our children are His children too, chosen by God to be with Him forever. Jesus came for all to be saved.

Pray every day for your children; turn their salvation over to God. Live lives that bring glory to God. Teach the children God's ways, and they will honor God. Be good examples for them and be a righteous person. Obey God's commands. Live your lives to honor God, and your children will truly be blessed.

Rest in the Lord

Is there quietness in the midst of confusion? Everyone is scurrying around me and looking for their place on this earth. Everyone is on the move going here and there without direction. Sometimes I feel like I am living in a crowded mall with people everywhere, bumping and shoving me from one side to another. Life goes so fast I can hardly keep track. How can I slow down? How can I find a resting place?

> I need God's guidance. Through His word I find the way. Show me your ways, O Lord teach me your paths; guide me in your truth and teach me, for my hope is in you all day long.
>
> Psalm 2:4–5

I needed to rest in the word and learn to follow God's lead. I needed my life to stay peaceful and not return to unrest. When everyone is scurrying, I want to be calm inside and peaceful.

I need to give control of my life to God. Jesus promised in the book of John when He left,

> Peace I leave with you, my peace I give you; I do not give to you as the world gives. I give unto you. Do not let not your heart be troubled and do not be afraid.
>
> John 14:27

This is where I want to be. I want to feel safe and rest in God's presence. There is such joy in His every word. I receive peace in my heart when He speaks to me through that word. Every page of the Bible shows me Christ; every page is full of blessings.

The only rest I receive is when I am surrendered completely. My body is like an empty shell to be filled with the Lord. I become complete when I am surrendered. God wants to live His life through me, His way. There is a lot of scripture God gave me telling me that He wants to fill my life with Himself. God wants to make me the person He planned for me, to be before I was born. When I was in His mind before I was conceived, God was thinking about me. In Isaiah, He says,

Whether you turn to the right or the left, your ears will hear a voice behind you, saying, "this is the way; walk in it."

Isaiah 30:21

I need to release my pride and give it up. I need to stop controlling my life and start living in God's will and not my will. The Bible says,

In all your ways acknowledge Him, and He will make your paths straight.

Proverbs 3:6

I needed to let Him direct me. What a good guide in life, someone who knows my future. I needed to remember, He is with me all the time, and yet I was living as if no one knew what I was up to. When I meditated on this, I realized I was disappointing God with all my ways. I just needed to live His way.

God has all our answers to all our questions in His word. He says,

I will instruct you and teach you in the way you should go; I will counsel you and watch over you.

1 Peter 5:7

God wants to lead me and teach me, all He wants is for me to ask for help from Him. Was I ready for an instructor who would only instruct me to go to good places and do good things and live for others? I would have to give up living the self-centered life I was living. Was I truly ready to be made new?

I surrendered my will to the will of God one October day and I became God's child. I wasn't His part time; I became His all the time. I received the peace that passes all understanding. My life became a life lived for the Almighty. I was made new. When God became the Lord of my life, I learned to trust Him and believe His holy word. I learned to trust the Lord with my life.

Peace on Earth

The holidays are over and the trees are down, and the hustle and bustle has stopped. I am home alone again. Thirty parties and Christmas events, forty people fed and entertained in my home. What fast fun I had. The last I remembered it was Thanksgiving, and we were carving the turkey and eating burnt gravy. Then there was this big flash, there were bells, and I heard music.

This is how every Christmas is around here. I start buying the presents at Halloween and setting up the trees at Thanksgiving, because I know there will be no time to enjoy shopping or baking before Christmas arrives. I want to prepare my heart for the Christ Child to arrive. I want to focus on the true meanings of Christmas. At most of the places I went, people didn't care much if He was born. I did, I cared.

His birth brings great joy to my life. A surge of excitement runs through my body when I remember that He has come for me to be set free, free from all my sin. So precious, so small, so innocent, He came on Christmas to save me, a grown-up, old, sinful person. He knew all the time he came, to save me.

Mary and Joseph knew that he was special. The shepherds came, they knew. Yet when I go out among the holiday people, they don't know. Christ is Christmas; He is what it's all about. Can't they see, don't they know Jesus is the one who came to save us all? The Bible says,

> Glory to God in the highest, and on earth peace to men on whom his favor rests.
>
> Luke 2:14

This time of the year should be a time of peace on earth instead of all the hustle and bustle that fills the air, and little is heard of Jesus.

We see big displays that say Peace on Earth, we receive cards that say Rejoice, and yet the peace and rejoicing are hard to find. Santa is everywhere, on all the street corners, on all the wrapping paper, and the children's eyes delight at his name. People say he is the true spirit of Christmas. Santa brings the twinkle in the children's eyes when Jesus should be the twinkle in everyone's eye, because eternal life is the best gift of all. I guess everyone thinks Jesus won't mind if they put Santa first till the kids grow up. You hear people say Christmas just isn't Christmas without little children around. But there is always a little baby named Jesus every Christmas, to bring you the true spirit of Christmas.

Can't they see? Don't they know? What will open their eyes? I love to be in church during this month, thinking, praying, and focusing on Jesus the Christ Child. Next year will be different; I will shop on the 4th of July, write out cards in August, bake cookies in September, and decorate them in November. I will give Him all my attention and spend as much or more time with my Lord, as I spend with my friends. I will rest in His promise of peace on earth that includes my own home. I will receive this infant into my home to show us the true meaning of Christmas. I don't want the Christmas story to be just a story; I want it to be real to my family and me. Jesus is real. He really came, He really died, He really rose, and He will really return for me one day.

Good Will People

And suddenly a great company of the heavenly host appeared with the angel, praising God and saying, "Glory to God in the highest, and on earth peace, to men on whom his favor rests."

Luke 2:13–14

During the Christmas season, cards, television, and billboards advertise the familiar words of Luke 2: "On earth peace, good will toward men." Everyone wants to have peace and good will toward men. It is the time of year when people are kind to one another. They give gifts to people and send cards of cheer to one another. They help and care for each other because this is the season of good will.

After the holidays are over many people suffer depression. They are no longer concerned about good will toward men. They are concerned about their own lives. They seem to no longer care about each other and have trouble acting like the "the good will people" of the Christmas season. They wonder, "What is my purpose on this earth?" It seems that many people search for the answer to that question. They look in books and ask their friends, "Why am I here? What is my purpose on this earth?" They seek the answer that will change their lives.

The angels knew their purpose. The angels praised God and gave Him the Glory. We need to realize our purpose on this earth. This verse speaks of our purpose, when it says, "Glory to God in the highest." Our purpose is to bring God Glory, just like the Son of God did when He was on earth; He gave all the glory to God. If we praise God in all we do and say, making Him the center of our lives, obeying His command to love one another, wouldn't we be the good-will people of the Christmas season, every day?

MARK 3:16

"These are the twelve he appointed"

Jesus called twelve men. They were from different backgrounds and different parts of the country. He chose them to walk with Him and minister to the people. We too are called to minister to the people in various ways. What did God call you to do? Are you heeding the call? Do you go where God sends you?

We need to give our lives and time to God. He will use you if you give Him permission to be used. He is waiting for you to permit it. Is your life yours or His?

He is calling you to serve Him, maybe in Sunday school, or to a nursing home or hospital. Maybe you are to just tell everyone you meet about the Savior of the world. Do you sing or serve? Are you gifted for hospitality? There is a ministry for you and God will gift you for it. Submit to God and His plan for you.

MASTER'S PLAN

The burning inside of me was like a fire, strong and piercing deep inside my heart. My heart said, "Give a retreat for ladies of your church." Every time I prayed, these thoughts filled my heart. So I prayed, "Lord, what do you want? We never have retreats at our church, Lord. We never meet like this in my church. Lord, what do you want me to do?" My prayers went up to heaven asking God to guide my way. This was unfamiliar water, an uncharted course. I concluded that this must be what God wanted because it was in my thoughts daily. I surrendered it to God and promised to trust and follow His lead.

God began His work the second Wednesday in May 1998. I was at Bible Study Fellowship when Teresa was chatting about her busy weekend. I sat with Teresa for nine months, and I thought I knew her. Teresa said, "This weekend while I was speaking at a retreat." My ears couldn't believe what they just heard and I said, "You speak at retreats?" Her answer was yes. My eyes turned to heaven, and a big *thank you* sailed up through the ceiling into God's Holy presence. This was it! He made the desire and now He would provide the speaker for this retreat; He was going to provide everything. From that moment on, I began to trust Him with this retreat, knowing it would be excellent, if I would only trust Him with all matters and follow His guidance.

As the summer months brought joy to my heart, God was still in charge. I ordered some materials through our women's missionary league at church, all kinds of skits, plays, devotions, and Bible studies. Among the items I ordered was a thick group of stapled papers called, "Journey to Faith - A Trip of a Lifetime." I began reading, and I knew God was making His plans, perfect, just perfect! This was a full packet of retreat material. Everything that we needed for the retreat was there, right down to the nametag design. There is very little work to do when God is in charge. I continued to pray for guidance and for God's control of me.

Now, the big step of faith was to present this to the pastor for approval. To my surprise, he encouraged me. I told him I thought this would be the most wonderful event the women of our church would ever experience. I put an article in the newsletter for women of faith to help plan this retreat. Nine women responded to the call, all very excited and ready to meet new challenges. These women were not afraid of the unknown. When we gathered, we prayed. We only met eight times, and prayer was an important part of these meetings. I felt I needed to trust God completely to be a good example to the others. We made prayer lists and prayed for everything we could think of, even the weather.

This retreat was bathed in prayer, and our prayers showed our trust in God's control; we needed His control over every little detail. We wanted this retreat to be spiritually uplifting for everyone who attended, and we needed the spirit to be present at all levels of planning. God allowed me to attend events that resulted in the selection of three other speakers and our singers. He gave us all of our ideas for the decorations, favors, and skits. We prayed and God provided it all.

One day, I went to the mailbox and there was a large envelope. Inside were two songbooks and one CD. I played the CD music and put the books in my office; this had all come to me free. I often take advantage of free offers, so I thought very little about my good fortune. One month to the day, I received another songbook and one more CD with a bill this time. I concluded I must have joined a CD Club. Surprise! I quickly gathered all songbooks, CD's, and correspondence and began to read and play the CD's. What a marvelous God we have. He plans everything, and when He plans it, it is excellent. These were the most beautiful songs I had ever heard. I stopped to thank God for the retreat songs. Then I opened the songbooks. (God is excellent.) There among the pages of notes to all the songs were overheads ready to be reproduced. This was exactly what we needed.

Four months before this retreat took place, my committee asked me how many I thought would attend. I thought and searched my heart and said, "I think there will be eighty." I did a lot of printing ahead, and we made some favors. We ordered some special gifts for each lady who attended. Everything we did, we did with the number eighty in mind. I just knew that would be the number, just like I knew this was the event I should put all my time and energy into. God calls us to follow Him, and He will make our way easy. The day of the retreat the registration was exactly eighty.

My health is not good, but I knew God would provide good health for me when I needed it. For over twenty years I have suffered from MD, and now the test for me really came. Would I be able to stay on my feet for the retreat, and did I trust God with my health? Could I keep stress free so I didn't become ill? The day of the retreat I felt so calm and so healthy. Oh, I wasn't perfect, but in my past years this could be considered perfect in comparison. I had to trust God with my whole self since this was truly a growing experience for me, and God was with me all the way.

I thought this retreat was for the ladies of my church, but the registration came in slowly and as I was praying about attendance, I felt I should open it up to the ladies of my community. So I invited ladies from our town and surrounding areas. The word got out and fifty of the ladies who attended were not from my church. God wanted this retreat to be for all ladies.

There were too many things that happened to tell you all of them, but God was present everywhere. With extra help from God, the hotel came with a large discount on the overnight rooms for the ladies and a $2000 hall rental forgiven, hundreds of dollars were donated to the retreat, and there was great food at a great price. For everyone who came, God gave them a lot for their small registration fee.

God always gives us more than we ask for. I can tell you it was all God wanted it to be, and He alone gets all the glory and praise. It was a very good retreat and the spirit of God touched every woman's life. The ladies who came spent a total of twenty-four hours in the presence of God the Father, God the Son, and God the Holy Spirit. This was truly the master's plan.

In 1999, I planned the first retreat named "Journey to Faith, a Trip of a Lifetime." We all dressed up like sailors and there was a giant Styrofoam twenty-foot paddle wheeler as the backdrop with small Styrofoam paddle wheelers on each table. This was a two-day retreat with lots of meal planning and hauling things to the hall where it was held. There was a lot of physical work, but my committee of nine had husbands and pickups to help us.

This retreat was to help us get a relationship with the Lord. It was to help us know what He wants us to do. We learned that we should put God first, spend time with Him, and pray. At the end of the retreat a sixty-year-old woman came to me and said, "I have been in church all my life and never knew I was supposed to tell others about Jesus. I always thought it was the pastor's job." I knew no matter how much work went into a retreat; it was worth it all if one person came to have the desire to share the good news about Jesus.

"In the Potter's Hands" was our second retreat and it was about being molded and shaped by God to be used. We learned how He wants to be there for us and how we want to be held in His powerful hands. The first two retreats I wrote out in long hand with my pencil because I could not use a computer yet; pages and pages of writing and hours and hours of work, all worth it because it was the Master's plan.

For that second retreat, I started praying in June of 1999, and it was held in February of 2000. This was a two-day retreat and 188 women attended; only about thirty were from my church. There were all denominations represented because we are all one body. I still was writing everything out in long hand, and that left the records of this retreat slim. It was a retreat about being held in the hands of the potter to be used by Him. There were skits and speakers and singers. Some of the ladies from the retreat attended our church the following Sunday and sat in the balcony and sang songs from the retreat. What a blessing we all received.

On June 1, 2000, I prayed about the next retreat and had no ideas on the theme, so there was no retreat. I gave the remaining seed money to church and closed the checking account thinking that was the end. I thought that was the last of the retreats because I did not have any desire to have any more.

My father became ill in August. He went to the hospital for two months and spent time on a ventilator and in October, I got diabetes and high blood pressure. I did not tell my family till December because of my dad being so ill, and everyone had enough on their plate without worrying about me. In December, I told my family because I went on three insulin shots a day and was consumed with regulating my blood sugar numbers. By February of 2001, I was in no shape to have a retreat. I was trying to get well, and my dad and mom was in great need of me. God knows our future, and He kept me from having extra stress when I was ill. What would my life have been like if I would have gone out on my own and had a retreat anyway just because we always had one.

I prayed every June to see if there would be any more retreats. In 2002, our pastor was leaving, and everyone was upset. When I prayed that summer, I knew we should have another retreat. It was to be called, "Held by Your Love." I prayed about a speaker and thought I was to ask my Avon district manager to be our speaker, so I called her. She had just found her birth mother and five siblings who did not know the Lord and through her love they, all came to know the Lord. It was a story of abuse and alcoholism. But she said it was too soon and could not speak about it yet. She gave me the number of Myrna Etheridge who was a speaker in a town thirty miles away. I called her, and she said she had been praying to have a retreat in our area for two years but did not have time on her own to put one together. I gave her the date I had picked out, and she looked at her calendar.

She told me she was an author of many books and she often hosted a Christian TV program in Illinois. She was a missionary to Haiti and other third world countries telling people about Jesus. She said her calendar was very full of speaking engagements and traveling out of the country. As she flipped through her calendar, she spoke with amazement as she said, "That weekend is the only weekend for six months I had open."

Myrna's story was one of a mother who lost her only two sons to cystic fibrosis four months apart, a failed marriage that followed, and how she was held in God's love to get through it all. Myrna spoke of how God transformed her into the servant He always wanted her to be and how she made it through with the help of God. Now she spends her life telling others of Jesus and His love.

My son, who gave me his computer, blessed this retreat, and I learned how to use it; that saved time and gave me better records. My typing skills came back very fast as I stayed up late at night typing and got up early to type some more. God knew what I needed and he provided. My committee was now a committee of five, but we were all working for the same goal and that was to help others to mature in Christ.

This retreat was about evangelism and how we should share our faith with others; with Myrna's background in mission work, her speech perfect. We decorated the meeting room with a babbling brook and beautiful clouds and trees as they entered which reminded us of heaven. In the back of the room, was a giant sign with the retreat logo and the name of the retreat.

We had an evangelism exercise at the end of the retreat that helped them to realize how urgent it is to tell others about Jesus. While I was explaining the rules of the game, my committee removed the giant sign in the back of the room. Behind it was a depiction of hell with Mylar flames six feet tall; it was dark and furious. The game went like this: I would read off an index card the plan of salvation from the Gospel to someone, then we two would go out and read an index card to someone else. Then they would get a card and read it to someone else. There were two, then four, then six, and so on.

The ladies understood the concept of sharing the Gospel with others. But in my game there was a hitch, one that would help them to feel the urgency of sharing. As they played the game, I would announce that the game must stop and with heaven in the front and hell in the back of the room I said, "There has just been a bus wreck and every one with a one on their name tag just died. If you heard the gospel and were saved, you may go to heaven. If you did not hear it today, you must go to hell." There were ropes blocking off heaven and hell so you had to stand in the middle of it. The ones in heaven were ok, but the ones in hell look frightened.

The ladies began to understand what was going on, and the ones who had not heard started calling out, "Tell me, tell me." There were plane crashes and earthquakes and fires and illness, all kinds of tragedies. The numbers on their nametags became so important to them, as they did not want to die. Then I made the disasters closer and closer, they came faster and faster and the feeling of urgency filled the room. Ladies began to run to one another reading the index cards to save one another. When the exercise was complete everyone was in heaven or hell, and the ladies all knew how important it was to tell everyone about Jesus as we looked at our friends in hell and realized there is certainly not enough time, so we must hurry. God's hands were all over this retreat once more; He was in control.

This retreat was designed to help the ladies know why they were on earth and how they could make a difference for Christ. Its purpose was to awaken the servant's heart that dwells in us, and to share the good news of Jesus Christ. We are to serve God out of joy and deep gratitude for what he has done for us. We gained a deeper understanding that we are healed to help others to know Christ, blessed to be a blessing, saved to serve.

The retreat in 2004's theme was picked because of the song, "God Will Make a Way." This retreat was a study of trouble; everyone has trouble in his or her life. We learned that God has a way out of our trouble, or He will be with us in the midst of it. We learned that God wants us to have peace and joy at all times, even in troubles. We learned to change our attitude about trouble and look for the blessing in our lives during them.

I wanted my former pastor to be our speaker. We were still without a pastor and he agreed to speak. Two months before the retreat, he cancelled because of knee surgery. I went to my knees asking God to provide another speaker. That week, I went to a men's clothing store to buy a button extender for my husband's dress shirt. The clerk reached over to get the extender from the shelf when a CD fell off the shelf. The clerk, a friend, said, "Oh, Pat, you would like this Christian tape by Tony Becker. She writes her own songs and they are great. I think she lost her son or something and wrote these songs." I bought the CD and went home to listen. Her songs were moving, and I knew I wanted her to speak for us. I called her and said, "Tony, I am Pat Renner, and I hold Christian retreats in Cape Girardeau, Missouri. I was wandering if you ever considered speaking and singing at a retreat?" She told me she was not only a singer, but also a speaker, and just got home from a four-day retreat where she was the main speaker. She agreed to speak and sing at this retreat.

She did not lose a son; she had infertility problems and miscarried many times. Her songs reflected the pain of wanting children and losing them before they were born. But she knew God would make a way for her, and He did because now she has two sons. By God's grace, she was healed.

When I prayed about the 2005 retreat, time came to mind. How could we make our days longer and our lives not so cluttered with all the things we do? It was about time management and organization. If we could spend more time in God's word, we would be less stressed; if our prayer life would increase, the pressure would decrease. If we could find more time to serve God every day, we should not experience the frustration of ineffective days.

The purpose of this retreat called, "Make your Day Count," was to know who gave us our time and who should have charge over it. This retreat was a two-day event; there were two different singing groups, a soloist, skits, three meals, and three speakers. The speakers blessed us by telling us how to manage our time, how to be women of excellence, and how to let God have control. The true value of life, as well as the quality of our faith, is measured not by how many years we live, but by what we do. Jesus said,

By their fruits you will recognize them.

Matthew 7:16

The women who came to this retreat discovered the real joy and deep satisfaction that comes from a controlled life, dedicated to the cause of Christ, and they learned to make their days count.

In 2006, I wanted to have a retreat about prayer. I wanted the ladies to know how God answers prayers, how we should pray, and the promises from God about prayer. I wanted them to know how important prayer is and how God wants us to praise and worship Him through prayer, not just pleading and asking for help. I wanted them to know that we should all have a prayer life, a living and active prayer life.

I prayed for a speaker for months and none rose up. During the summer, I read three books about prayer and was so inspired. I highlighted the parts that moved me. Still no speaker came to mind. During my prayer time in October, I knew who the speaker would be. I got my daughter-in-law to be the MC for the retreat called, "Lord, Teach us to Pray." I was to speak the words of the authors. I took the highlighted sections and put them together as book reports for the ladies in three different session times, these were words from women of God who really know prayer. I tied them all together with my words, inspired by God, and words from the Bible, and the Lord did teach us to pray that year.

Love was to be the theme of the 2007 retreat, not just any kind of love but "A 13–13 kind of love."

And now these three remain: faith, hope, and love. But the greatest of these is love.

1 Corinthians 13:13

We learned how God wants us to love and serve one another, with compassion and the love that dwells within us through the Spirit. The Lord blessed us by teaching us how to pray.

In 2008, the Retreat title was, "You Are the Light of the World," and we learned that we were the light that could share the message of Jesus with others. We learned how God's amazing peace could shine brightly around us so we could always see God's amazing love. We are all lighthouses standing strong and firm waiting to guide others to Christ. We are a witness for Christ alone.

In June of 2008, I prayed once more and knew for sure there would be a retreat that year, and by September, it was finished and scheduled for February 7, 2009. I was amazed that all of it, even the little details, was completed: registration envelopes stuffed, meals picked out, and speakers acquired. Very little work went into this retreat it just fell together by God's grace. God always knows our future, and He is in control of it all. October 3rd, 2008 I had a car wreck.

This car wreck would devastate my life for years. I was off my feet for three months. I went from a wheelchair, to a walker, and then a cane. Recovery was slow, and I still use the cane today. I broke my ankle, but then acquired RSD, reactive sympatric dystrophy. RSD was the most pain I had ever had in my life.

When the retreat came, I had the wheelchair, walker, and cane by my side. I could barely get to the podium to speak. The name of this retreat God planned ahead was, "In Moments Like These." It was for ladies who were tired and weary, with special needs like me. With pom-poms in hand, Christie, my daughter-in-law, dressed as a cheerleader and led us in cheers throughout the day for the victory we found.

I knew God sent the ladies who attended the retreats because He planned this retreat just for them. At this retreat, 30 percent of the ladies attending were there for the very first time and twenty of the ladies came by themselves, which was unusual since ladies almost always go together with friends. Ladies with a great need came to learn how to live in moments like these.

We always had a book table with books about the retreat topic available to buy. The singer in 2009 was a member of the Zoe Girls, a well-known Christian singing group. Her songs blessed us all, and we learned to walk out of the darkness into God's marvelous light in moments like these. It was ten years since I started having retreats, and I praise God He selected me to have them.

The speaker I picked out six months before the retreat was Hazel Kinder from Columbia, Missouri. She told the story of her life with three children that were born with neurological degenerative disease. She spoke of how they all died before they were seven. She was their nurse day and night for eleven years, before they were all called home to heaven. How could anyone go home with self-pity or depression because her life wasn't going right? Was my broken ankle a problem? No! Was I going to get on with my life in spite of not walking well? Yes! This retreat was for me too.

God knows us, and He loves us, and He plans our future. The retreats took place because of prayer, and I gave them totally to the Lord to control. If we place our trust in the Lord, He is always there. His love for us comes down from heaven and out through us to others. We learned how God goes with us through all the storms and will take us to the other side of them, always.

In 2010, there was no retreat, but I am writing this book; so that must be His plan for me today.

JOHN 3:16

"For God so loved the world that he gave his one and only Son, that whoever believes in him shall not perish but have eternal life."

This is love: that someone would give up their child so that others may live. That is surprising, but even more surprising is that they would do this for you and for me; we do not deserve this kind of grace.

When we take a good look at our lives all we see is self-centeredness. We want everything it is all for us, and about us. We want to be first, to lead the life we planned not the life God wants for us. We accept His death for us but we do not want to give Him His rightful place in our lives because of that death.

Jesus wants to be your all in all. He wants to be first, He wants to be your Lord, and He wants you to be Christ-centered. Humble yourself and follow His call and serve him for the rest of your life.

GOD AT WORK IN ME

God is always watching over me and using me, but I always realized that He is there. I always looked for God at work once I knew He was active in my life. I always acted upon any calling I had. What kind of woman was I becoming? I was changing all the time, and my life was full of the presence of God.

"Mr. and Mrs. Renner, please stand in front of the alter," he said, "We want your pictures before the wedding." We stood in the front of the church as people gathered to attend the wedding of our son, Scott. As a mother, I could sense my son's despair. All these feelings were not wrong because the marriage lasted one year and one month. She had a new boyfriend and was gone out of our lives forever. Scott told us later he almost didn't show up for the wedding but came because of the relatives and all the preparations that were made for this day.

God uses all our events to promote his Kingdom. His plan this day was for Scott to get married, so I could have my picture taken at his wedding. It was the only picture I was in, so I didn't get to know the photographer at all. As I said, God has a plan for your life and mine and even for John, the photographer's life.

At the wedding, my pastor spoke to John and invited him to go to church at Hanover, as he was new in town. John was angry at his church and no longer attended and was losing faith in God. After the wedding on Sunday morning, I fixed breakfast for thirty-one of the relatives before they left town to go back home. I didn't go to church that morning, but the next Sunday I was back. I went to my pew; you know the pew that could have your name on it as it had all your fingerprints. This pew was the third pew on the right, and my seat was the second seat, and Gib's was the first. When I sat down, there was John the photographer in the third seat right next to me.

This is the time you can visibly see God's presence, and His plan began. Now it was up to me to respond. I looked at John and said, "You are the photographer?" He said, "Yes, I'm John." When God has a plan, there is nothing we can do but react to it. I didn't know the plan God had for John until Easter of 1995, when it was complete.

Every Sunday thereafter, John sat right by me in church. We became friends, and I found out John was in town alone working six days a week. His wife-to-be was in Wisconsin. I adopted John as a third son and had him over on Sunday's for dinner, and we would talk and get to know one another.

A month after we met, my husband invited John to haul hay with him and the boys after church. You know you make hay while the sun shines in our house. John was eager to come and help. He had never hauled hay before. What fun we had that day. I drove the tractor, and all the boys pitched bales. When the hay was done, I invited John home for supper. Scott, the newlywed, wanted to go home to his new wife, and Tim had something to do with his buddies. So it was just the three of us for supper. John was very hungry after such hard work. When we finished eating, Gib left the kitchen, and it was just John and me.

In my life, I know God wants me to tell others about Him, and I never pass on that opportunity. When He opens the door, I tell others of Christ. John and I began talking, and John said, "Tell me about your Jesus." That was my opportunity. I told him how Jesus came to earth to die just for him and that believing in Him, John could have eternal life and would never die but would live forever in heaven. I told him I knew for sure because God's Word to us, the Bible, said all this.

John asked a lot of questions and with help from the Holy Spirit, I could answer all his questions that night. I was sowing seed for Christ, and there were seeds all over my kitchen that night. John was the fertile soil, and now God would water and tend to His seeds, and they would grow.

Time passed, and John got married and brought his new wife, Tina, to Cape. She was my adopted child too; they were a joy to know. They would join us at the lake and go on hayrides with us in the fall and had us over for dinner. They would sit with us in the third pew at church every Sunday.

John grew in Christ. He joined a men's Bible study and read God's word daily. John became close friends with our pastor; he would soak up the wisdom of God through the sermons. John became a strong, dynamic, Christian man. On Easter Sunday, 1995, John and Tina told us John was taking a new job out of town and they were moving the next week. We still hear from them by mail.

I thank God for John; he was a joy God put in my life. God is in control of all of our lives at all times, even if we don't know it. My son had to have that wedding, with pictures, John the photographer was the one God planned for my son to hire. Pastor had to invite him to church; John had to choose the seat next to mine. John had to haul hay and be hungry, and I had to ask him to dinner. I had to love God enough to tell John about Him. I sowed and God watered and there was a harvest.

God teaches us a lot through our life circumstances, and we should pay attention to the lessons, so we do not have to learn them again. I learned a big lesson one week about how comforting the knowledge of eternal life was for me.

The week began on a Friday night when my husband's cousin, by marriage, died with cancer. Months of suffering, and now his family felt relief because he was set free from the pain. His five children and wife gathered together to mourn his passing. Paul was a man of faith. He knew Jesus, and he was heaven bound. Paul and his family were being prayed for every day all over town, and they realized the power in prayer, because peace surrounded them at this time.

On Saturday morning, Elise died. She was the oldest member of our church at ninety-seven. She was in fairly good health for a woman of her age, but she started to fail and had to go to the nursing home. Day-by-day her health failed, and she became weaker and weaker until she peacefully went home to heaven. Lizzie, as we called her, was a woman of great faith, and her life reflected Jesus' presence. She never married and had great love in her life for God. She was an example of faithfulness.

On Sunday night, we went to the funeral home for Paul. There were lines that led out the front door waiting to pay their respects. Paul was a businessman in town and was loved by all who knew him. Betty, his wife, stood right by his casket all night. His children and spouses were there too. Paul was only sixty-seven; he was thirty years younger than Lizzie. On Monday, I got up bright and early and prayed for the families to have comfort in their time of loss. At ten o'clock, I picked up my friend, and we went to Paul's funeral. His eight best friends sat and waited to carry him to his final resting place. The priest spoke of Paul's faith in God even to the end. I dropped off my friend and went to Lizzie's funeral. The songs were about great love for the Lord. I realized God has a plan for each of our lives, and he loves us more then we will ever know.

On Tuesday morning, the top local news story was an eighteen year old, Jessica, killed in car wreck. I didn't know her, but I knew her parents. We had spent weekends with them on trips and her mother was my "Little Sister" in sorority when we were young. Jessica's aunt and uncle live next door to us. When I heard the news, I fell to my knees, once again, in prayer to comfort the parents and family. I asked the Lord to give them strength to get through this.

Her death came fast. There was no time to think, no time to prepare. It was a sudden death; she was taken like a thief in the night. Jessica's parents will never forget her, they will love her and think about her until they are together again in heaven.

Every day there seemed to be death all around me. When Wednesday came, I hesitated to open the newspaper. There was Glenn's name he had a heart attack he was sixty-four. Glenn was in the band that played at our wedding thirty years ago, and his wife was one of my Avon customers now.

Thursday there was another name I recognized in the obituaries, Dru, one of our friend's grandchildren. He had leukemia since he was two years old and was only nine years old when he died. It had been in arrest for many years, but it returned. I guess there will be one more visit to the funeral home, and one more family crying. These events in my life reflected death, but I learned a lot about life this week.

This week, I realized how precious life is no matter what the age, ninety-seven or nine. This could be our last day on this earth, and we should live life fully for the Lord. I realized that when we speak of eternal life, it really means a lot to the ones we love and the ones left when we die. Lizzie knew about eternal life, that is why she was happy to go to heaven with her Lord. She had no fear of death. Jesus rules over death, sin, and the devil, and he has saved us. There is no more death, only life. Believing in Him no matter the age nine, eighteen, sixty-four, sixty-seven, or ninety-seven, you can live in God's kingdom forever. Believe these promises of God, and you will live.

1 CORINTHIANS 3:16

"Don't you know that you yourselves are God's
temple and that God's Spirit lives in you?"

In the Old Testament the temple was a building where God dwelled. There the High Priest gave sacrifices as atonement for sin. Today the Holy Spirit of God dwells in us. This happened because of Jesus. He left this earth when He ascended into heaven to sit at God's right hand. He left us His Comforter.

If we are the temple of the living God why then do we act like the world? Every time we act like the world, saying or doing ugly things we take the Spirit of Jesus Christ with us. Do we realize He is there? Would we act different if we would remember the Holy Spirit never leaves us after we are saved? Wouldn't we make better choices if we realized we are God's *temple? Live life with the knowledge of God's presence all the time.*

THE DARKEST HOURS

My life was not always full of peace; there were dark hours of despair too. I didn't have many dark times, but I did have them. I did learn how to stay out of the darkness as I matured in Christ and tried not to be in those times. I don't like to talk about those times, because they bring me down when I remember. These are hours when it took me longer to turn to God, the hours I felt alone, but He was always there. I used the pain and loneliness that overcame me to witness in my jail ministry, and I believe I understood those girls' despair because I had it too. I think all women have times of loneliness and times in the darkness.

I didn't cry much in my life, but when I finally did, it was moments of grieving. I never liked to cry because I believe it would lead me into a state of self-pity that I did not want or like. When I was a young wife and mother, I would cry because of loneliness. I felt lonely a lot, even when my husband and two boys would be sleeping in their beds.

Once, I was crying in my bathroom in the middle of the night alone. The window was open, and I was weeping and talking out the window trying to fill the void I had in my lonely life. I guess I was praying but didn't realize it because I did not know Jesus intimately yet. While I was crying I came to realize I was not alone. God promised He would always be with me and never forsake me or leave me. That night changed my life.

I remember another night when I was feeling lonely and crying in the basement so no one would hear. Timmy woke up and came down to see where I was. He was about eight years old and comforted me. He said he loved me, and I was not alone because he was with me.

I remember my Timmy would call my mom at night and say, "Grandma, I am all alone." She would reply, "Where is your mommy?" He would say, "At a meeting." Then Grandma would ask, "Well, where is your daddy?" Timmy said, "He is sleeping." Then she would say, "Where is your brother?" Timmy would reply, "He is sleeping too, I'm all alone." I know how he felt. I didn't call anyone, I just wept.

Women can be lonely in a crowd. Women want to be needed and wanted and loved; we want to never feel lonely. As women, we want someone to care about us and be involved in our lives. We want to talk it out in the middle of the night.

Gib was not a talker. We never really talked about much, just the necessary agenda of the day. And he liked to talk about guy stuff so we did.

When people read this book, they will learn things about me they never knew before. That is why I wanted to write this book because no one really knows about me or what I did day-by-day. I really didn't mind not speaking about the things I did for Christ because God knew all about me. I pray this book will help someone to learn how to live for the Lord and have joy and peace in their lives.

My health is so bad and has been for over thirty-four years. That contributed to my darkest moments, and I only have brief times of relief. I pretend to be well, and I am thankful to be alive, but when I have those dark times, I envy people that can walk, or run. I watch people who can work and be productive in their lives. I marvel at the people of endurance who can go on and on all day without tiring.

Every day is a challenge in my life, just to see if I can live another day without going to bed. Just to get through the day without giving out. I fight to stay on my feet and not give into the backache. The mall is a challenge, the parking lot is a challenge, and shopping, well it is only done in short trips.

I remember I was crying once and wrote down what I was crying about and hid the letter to be read at a later date when the darkness was gone. When I reread the letter a week later, it was about a sad, lonely women who needed to talk to someone. I called this letter my Poor Pitiful Patty Letter. I learned not to cry and be so sad from writing this letter, and I learned to turn to God first because He cares for me.

I hadn't cried for a long time until I broke my ankle in the car wreck, and I didn't cry because I had a broken ankle or because I had to stay in bed for months. But because Gib did not know what to do or how to take care of me, I cried. He is a good man but not a caregiver.

Now Gib needs a caregiver. Alzheimer's is now in our home; Gib was told he has begun the journey into memory loss. We knew something was happening to his memory for three years, so we lived fast and traveled a lot. We packed a suitcase once a month and went on a trip. We visited our friends and relatives and took trips out of the country. We cruised in oceans and watched the waves hit shores far from home. For three years, we behaved like this would be the last time we would ever travel because we knew the travel time was coming to an end. I wanted Gib to see all he could see and enjoy all there was to enjoy because he would not remember one day, but we have pictures to talk about.

I don't know our future, but I do know God will never leave us alone. I don't know if I can be the caregiver Gib will need, but God has given me the task. I am having trouble accepting my new season of life, and I will have to keep looking up and stay out of the darkness. God equips us to do all He gives us, and I will trust Him with my unknown future. Our life will be a life of depending on one another, with my physical disabilities and his memory loss; we will make one good person together.

I still spend a lot of time alone, and years ago I learned I am not alone but with God. This chapter of the darkness is not very long because I did not spend much time in that dark place in my life. I stayed in the light where Jesus is. I believe dwelling on the dark time in one's life is not good, and I almost did not write this chapter but life is not all good and peaceful. Life is not a bowl of cherries, everyone has difficult times, but during the darkness, I never doubted God at all. I never questioned why me? I always knew God loved me and wanted the best for me. People always disappointed me, but God never does.

HEBREWS 3:16

"Who were the people who heard God's voice and rebelled against him? All those who were led out of Egypt by Moses."

After 40 years Moses led the people out of Egypt. They spent their life disobeying God. They didn't listen to God. They were rebellious and did not believe so they went their own way; for forty years! Let that be a lesson to you. God wants children who believe in Him and who obey Him and do not turn away. God wants trusting children. God wants you to dwell with Him. He wants to have a relationship with you. Some people do wonder forty years before they come to know Jesus as their Savior. Is that the best way to just wander for years without the Lord?

You need to know the word of God and it will lead you into a relationship with Jesus that will last an eternity. Dwell in the presence of Christ and make Jesus the center of your life. Don't spend another minute wandering around without Him.

GET TO KNOW MY JESUS

There were times I needed God to handle my life, so I wrote about God and his love and strength in my life. The stories all started with a thought and ended with Jesus. They were about seeking the face of Jesus or about how He would never leave me alone. I wrote about how all my strength came from the Lord. When I write, a peace comes over me because I am in the presence of the Lord.

Love Letter

Dear Beloved,

If only I could let everyone know how much I love you. I love you more than anything on earth, more than life itself, more than diamonds and gold. I need you to always be in my life, I am nothing without you.

There was an empty place in my heart, then your love came into my life, and I know you love me too. I know I don't love you as much as you love me, because you told me so. I remember when you said I was precious to you and that you would love me forever and I believe you.

I think about you all the time and feel so safe. You make me so happy and my life with you is so peaceful. I love you, and I never want us to be apart. I know you want this too because you said you would always be near me and hear me when I call.

I can always rely on you to be there in my times of need. You bring such joy to my life; I want our love to last forever. One day, when I was sitting in the quiet of my room and reading what you wrote to me, you said, I belonged to You, and that You would never leave me or forsake me. I love you because you alone are my Lord and my Savior, you are my Jesus. Thank you for loving me first.

Eternally yours, Patty

Dear Friend

I wanted to write you and tell you about the God that I know. He is gracious, He loves and cares for me, and He strengthens me and brings power to my life. He promised me He would never leave me. I trust Him because He is trustworthy. He is my redeemer and my shepherd. He made a way to live with Him forever because He sent His Son to save me. Jesus died on the cross at Calvary as atonement for my sins. Because of this great love, I now have eternal life.

My God is three in one; He is the Father, the Son, and the Holy Spirit. The Father is almighty and powerful, He is larger than life. I feel small and meek in God's presence. When I think about God the Father, I visualize climbing up onto His lap to rest, as He sits on the throne with me cradled in His loving arms. He rocks me back and forth, as I rest in His protection and safety. God the Father wanted me to be His child before I was born.

The second in this Trinity is God the Son. Jesus is His name, and He is my friend. Jesus loves me more than anyone here on this earth will ever love me. He loves me with a perfect love. Whenever I feel sad and in trouble, Jesus wraps His loving arms around me, and He holds me tight. He will never let me fall.

He loves me so much he came to earth as a man and hung on a cross to forgive me and never complained. It was this act that set me free, free from the sin that binds me. He wants me to be like Him in every way, so He lived as an example to me. He is never angry, impatient, worried, guilty, or selfish. Jesus rose from the dead and returned to heaven where He lives now. When Jesus left this earth, He said He was going to make a place for me in heaven. And now, I want to read His word and learn His ways.

The Holy Spirit is the third part of the three-in-one. The Spirit was left here on earth with us the day Jesus returned to heaven. I believed that Jesus died for me, and the Holy Spirit of God entered me and lives in me now. The Holy Spirit leads and guides my steps. Through the Holy Spirit, I have power to do God's will and to love with an everlasting love. I have the gifts of the Spirit the Bible promised. I have the light of Christ in me, and now I have peace and joy in my heart and mind.

This knowledge and truth of God has changed my life. God the Father, Son, and Holy Spirit are the truth that guides my life. God wanted you to be His child before you were born too. May God's saving grace be yours. Love Patty.

When I was in the Christian writer's guild, we had an assignment to write about our fathers. It was around Father's day, and this was my writing about my Father.

My Father's Voice

Everyone who believes Jesus Christ died on the cross for their sins, was raised from the dead, and ascended into heaven, is saved. The Holy Spirit of God then comes in and dwells within them. Now they can hear the Father's voice.

God said,

> My sheep listen to my voice; I know them, and they follow me
> John 10:27

I am His sheep, and I can hear His voice when He calls my name in the quiet of the night. When He whispers to me in the silence of my thoughts, I hear God's voice through His Spirit. This voice is comfort and peace and joy to me.

I want to hear my Father's voice. I long to hear the voice of almighty God. The desire of my heart is for my innermost thought to be from Him. I need to hear His Words to me. God speaks to me through His word, the everlasting, infallible Word of God. His word is filled with instruction and direction on how to live and love. I learned how to live by His example. I learned to know the Savior of the world through His word.

He says in His word, I can have inexpressible and glorious joy. He tells me I can have the peace that passes all understanding. He says I am beautiful in His sight. He tells me I will never be alone, and He will never leave me. He says I am precious to Him. My Father's voice is beautiful.

I see my Father's voice through the magnificence of His creation. He speaks through the ocean depths. I can see Him in a rainbow and hear Him shout in the mountaintop echoes. God speaks to me through the seasonal changes, because my Father's voice is in everything I see.

My Father's voice leads my way and lights my path. He has prepared a way out of all unpleasant circumstances. I live every day seeking to hear my Father's voice.

Passion for Holiness

Jesus Christ had a passion for holiness. When He went to the temple and men were buying and selling sacrificial animals, He was angry. People were trying to pray in this Holy place. This place held the presence of God and they were defiling it and distracting the people's prayers. Jesus showed His righteous anger to the open disrespect of this Holy place.

We can understand Jesus' anger and agree that Jesus was right to keep this Holy place holy. Now we read in the bible,

Do you know that your body is a temple of the Holy Spirit, who is in you, whom you have received from God? You are not your own.

1 Corinthians 6:19

Like the defiling of the temple angered Jesus, how much more must it anger Him when we become defiled or distracted from Him? We are now the temples of the Holy Spirit. Our lives should reflect that Spirit. Our words should speak powerful words of God. Our eyes should be fixed on Jesus, as He alone is our Lord.

When the Holy Spirit indwells in us, we are more like Jesus. We are a new creation, the old self is gone, and a new self is born again in Christ Jesus. When we act like our old self, we defile the temple. When we don't trust God with our whole life, we are distracted from our prayers. Jesus wants all of our life, not just what we allow Him to have. He wants to use us to bring Himself glory. Jesus will not tolerate sin where holiness resides. He said to choose whom you will serve. Does holiness or sin reside in you?

When Jesus stands at your temple steps and looks deep into your heart, what does He see? Is your temple full of Him? Is there worship in your temple? Is fervent prayer going on unceasingly? Are all of your burdens cast upon Him, and have you surrendered all of your will to His will? Are you a humble servant ready to serve the one true God? The blood of Jesus Christ forgives you, and you are made pure white and holy. You are free from sin and are saved by grace alone. Jesus has a passion for holiness, and this same holiness He wants for you.

Hope of Glory

While we wait for the blessed hope, glorious appearing of our great God and our Savior, Jesus Christ.

Titus 2:13

Jesus is referred to as "blessed," and we realize that He truly is a blessing from God. He showers blessings on us. He has blessed us by saving us, teaching us, and loving us. He is the Son of God, the Redeemer of man. He is the best blessing any person on this earth could have. We are made pure and holy by His death on a cross. Could more love be shown by anyone?

Do we have hope in our lives? Do we have hope of living forever with Him in glory? Do we long for His return to be the King of Kings and Lord of Lords? Most of us don't live waiting for Christ's return. We live our lives absorbed in this world. We live looking forward to tomorrow and days filled with self. We live as if we are going to be here an eternity, yet we will die. So why do we live so permanently in such a temporary world?

When we are a saved and redeemed child of God, we know the impact of that day on Calvary. We realize Jesus' role in our life here on earth. He blessed us in many ways while He was here on this earth. He taught us how to live for Him. He taught us how to love with a love like no other love. He taught us how we should care for one another. He was truly a blessing from God, so we call Him blessed.

To live for Christ on this earth, to live in His presence, and to live to bring Him glory, produces in us the hope of glory. We will live with the hope of heaven and Christ's presence in our lives. When Christ is the center of our lives, we will long to be with Him in paradise. When Christ is the center of our lives, we will live obediently here on this earth. When He is what we live for, we will serve Him and no other gods. Every day we will long to be in His presence, by His side, close to His glory. The closer we are to Christ on earth, the more we will look to Him as our blessed hope in glory.

Merciful God

All have sinned and fall short of the glory of God.

Romans 3:23

We are all born sinners. That is what the Bible says. Our lives are lives headed only for despair, separated from God, and full of sin. We are certainly not worthy of anything good. We are not born with heaven in our future, but we are bound for hell the minute we come into this wicked world. We are just poor miserable sinners.

When we look at life with the truth in mind, heaven seems far from our grasp. Yet, some will go to heaven. Why? Because God is a God of mercy, grace, and love. He saves us from the doom we deserve. He sent His Son to die on a cross in our place. The punishment we deserved, He took upon Himself. God placed His holy hand on us and redeemed us from our pit of hell. He, in His mercy, saved us.

Some people ask, "Why did a loving God let my loved one die?" I say to them, "God is a loving God who saved them from the death they deserved." When we look at our lives through God's eyes, we see that He knew we were sentenced to hell. So, He gave up His Son for us. He did not let loved ones die; He let His loved one Jesus die in their place. Our God is a God of mercy. He loves all people, even poor miserable sinners.

Power of the Spirit

But you will receive power when the Holy Spirit comes on you; and you will be my witnesses in Jerusalem, and in all Judea and Samaria, and to the ends of the earth.

Acts 1:8

You will receive power. Do Christians really use the power they receive? Do we give God the complete use of our lives? These are real questions to ponder.

Our lives are crowded with doing useless things. We don't think God can accomplish great and mighty things through us. So we settle for living our lives for the world; going through the motions of life. At times, we look like Christians, yet, at other times, we look like people far from God. We live so much in the world and in it's ways, we look like the world. We need to release our lives to the power of the Holy Spirit, and let the Spirit of God have His way with us. We need to truly be set free from our old ways and become new creations. We can do this through the power of the Holy Spirit.

One way to do this is to let the Holy Spirit rule our lives and surrender to the will of God and worship Him. We should be obedient to His word. We should sing praises to Him. The Bible speaks of lifting up holy hand in praise and singing spiritual songs. We sing, "O come let us adore Him," but do we really take the time to do these things in worship of our Lord?

We need to walk in the power of the Holy Spirit we possess. With this power we will have discernment, knowledge, attributes of God, and the ability to love like Christ. He will be the good that lives within us. When we think of Jesus' sacrifice, do we realize the love He has for us? He gave us everything. We try to make a little time in our day to spend with Him. We give God an hour here and there in our week. We don't even think about Him moment by moment, when we are all that is on His mind.

We need to take time for God every hour of every day. He wants to walk beside us and be in our lives. He wants to consult with us in every decision. He loves each of us the most. Do we love Him the most? Who else loves us enough to give up His Son for us? Who else has given us such power, as the power of the Holy Spirit?

When the Holy Spirit of the Lord and Savior Jesus Christ comes upon each of us, we will tell everyone of His awesome grace for them. We won't be able to quiet our Spirits. God will be our constant companion. We will worship and praise Him, and speak of Him as often as we can. We will be made new by the power of the Holy Spirit.

Count It a Privilege

Christ brings life and light to a dead and dark world. The Bible says,

> But these are written that you may believe that Jesus is the Christ, the Son of God, and that by believing you may have life in His name.
>
> John 20:31

How many people lack this knowledge? John wants everybody to know Jesus. That was his goal. He counted it a privilege to tell others of Christ and His salvation for us. John's message is clear about Jesus. John was greatly used by God and you can be greatly used too.

I count it a privilege to be used by God. Are you one of the privileged? Does God use you to send His message into a hurting and dying world? God willingly uses us to send His message to the lost, but only if we are willing to be used. If you are not sharing the gospel with others, look deep into your own heart for the answer why.

How do you become bold enough to speak the words God has for His people? You accepted Jesus as your Savior and you now have the Holy Spirit dwelling in you. Why don't you share the Good News of Christ with everyone? Is it because of your own stubborn will? Are you too proud to surrender to God's will? Too proud to acknowledge that maybe you need help in what you do for God the Almighty? We now have the Holy Spirit dwelling in us yet we do not seem to have any power. Do you squelch the power by being powerful? Stop! Stop now, and ask the Holy Spirit to guide your way, lead you, and empower you.

You need to step out of God's way to allow the power to flow through you. The Holy Spirit will make you bold for Christ. You will have a burning desire to reach out to the unreached. People will see Christ in you. People will know a Savior because you counted it a privilege to be used by God and live life fully for the Lord.

I Keep My Eyes on Jesus

Today I learned a great lesson, and I want to share it with you. When I feel life is dark and gray, when there is evil all around, when I feel smothered by the sin in the world, I keep my eyes on Jesus. When people disappoint me, when no one will help me up when I fall, I keep my eyes on Jesus. When the world seems to have no humanity or love, only greed, and selfishness, I keep my eyes on Jesus. When I begin to get contempt in my heart, I feel myself becoming like them, and I keep my eyes on Jesus.

At these times, I look to the Lord and His word. God's world is not like what I spoke of above. His world is peaceful, calm, loving, and it is right here on earth.

> Trust in the Lord with all your heart and lean not on your own understanding; in all your ways acknowledge Him and He will make your paths straight.
>
> Proverbs 3:5–6

I know He saved me not only from my sin but also from the evilness of this earth. I cannot hide from it, but my heart and my mind can think about Jesus, and I can keep my eyes on Him.

> Do not be anxious about anything but in everything, by prayer and petition, with thanksgiving, present your request to God.

And the peace of God, which transcends all understanding, will guard you hearts and your minds in Christ Jesus.

Philippians 4:6–7

When I think about Christ, a calm comes over me. I can't express exactly how I feel, but I know I'm near to God, and I am sure He loves me. I don't feel like I am of this world when my eyes are fixed on Him.

When I go to sleep, I think about Him, and when I wake up, He is still in my thoughts. I move through each day like other people, but my mind is thinking about my Lord and His promises to me. I keep my eyes on Jesus.

Jesus

The world is still laughing and persecuting Jesus, just like the day He was crucified. People are still crucifying Jesus everyday with their words and actions.

They shut Him out of their lives. People still curse His name and the world hates Him.

Only a few love Him, only a few worship Him as the Christ and their Savior. But, like the disciples, they too run and hide from Him. When asked if they know Him, they deny any relationship with Him, because they feel threatened by the majority of unbelievers around them. We all are sinners and live for the world's pleasures. We all fall short of what God wants for us. God wants to have a relationship with us, and He wants us to be bold in our faith. He wants us to submit to Him.

Christ was rejected before He hung on that cross, and today that is the way we treat Him. We reject Him. We do not cry out, "Crucify Him," but we do not boldly tell others about His love for them. We do not witness to the unbelievers about this day on Calvary just for them.

If all is well with peace and joy in our lives, we call Him Lord. When conflict or turmoil comes, do we stand up confidently for Jesus, trusting Him with our whole life? Do we think God has left us when things start going wrong? People, even religious people, turned Jesus over to be crucified because the crowd wanted it. They turned away to let Him die. They didn't want to be associated with Him. They had a mob mentality and followed the world.

This is the time to stand up for Jesus. This is the time to hold His name above all names. He is the true Savior of the world and now is the time to proclaim His name. We need to have the same passion for Christ as He had for us. He gave us everything He had. He loved us above all things. He had such a passion for our lives He died for our sins. We need to love Him the way He loved us. We need to give up our lives to Him. We need to love Him above all others. He asks us to surrender to Him and serve Him; do we?

Passion comes for the indwelling Holy Spirit. When the Spirit lives in us, we have the power to love like Jesus. We have the ability to be faithful, and we can be bold in our witness for Christ. As long as we love the world more than we love Christ, we have no power or passion. We need to let go of the world and surrender to the Lord. Let Jesus be the one you live for. Jesus is truly the light of the world; carry His light.

Pass It On

He who has the Son has life; he who does not have the Son of God does not have life. I write these things to you who believe in the name of the Son of God, so that you may know that you have eternal life.

1 John 5:12–13

There are a lot of people I know who do not worship anywhere. I'm sure you know some too. I find when people don't worship; they just don't read the word of God either. 1 John 5: 12–13 probably is not in their file of very important things to know. This is a very sad thing that is happening all over the world; people don't read the word or worship the Almighty God. They are just sure they are all right because they lead an upright, good citizen life, filled with random acts of kindness.

He who has the Son has life. It is so simple. Anyone who can read it or hear it can have eternal life by only believing in Jesus. No other instructions given, only by believing do we receive.

Eternal life? Living forever, never dying? How can something so wonderful be so simple? We may die physically one day, but God promises all who believe in Jesus will never die. Isn't this worth praising and worshipping a God who loves us so much? All we have to do is believe that Jesus died to forgive us and rose from the dead to conquer Satan forever and ascended into heaven to secure a place for us. Sounds simple. So why do so many reject Jesus as their Savior? Because they didn't read the part in 1 John that says, "he who does not have the Son of God does not have life."

How will they know this, my friends and neighbors, if they don't read the word and if I don't tell them? Maybe God's plan was for each one of us to tell someone of God's marvelous plan, full of grace and mercy. That's it! I figured it out! I will tell you and you tell someone and they tell… it will go on and on, so no one is left without the Son of God and able to live eternally with Him.

I really love God and I am so thankful for what Jesus did for me, and I want to tell someone of God's love. Okay, I just told you about God's plan of salvation for you. Now you go tell someone and tell him or her to pass it on. It is truly up to us, you know!

EPHESIANS 3:16

"That he would grant you, according to the riches of his glory, to be strengthened with might by his spirit in the inner man."

We can always overcome and live in victory because of the indwelling Spirit of God. He gave us this power in our inner man called the Holy Spirit.

Do we realize what Jesus gave us when He left this earth to dwell in heaven?

Jesus called it the comforter. This presence living in us brings us comfort and peace.

We can truly have the peace that passes all understanding because of this indwelling spirit. We can live our lives as overcomers with the power we have to live through the trials of our lives. His Spirit helps to show us a way out of all difficulties. His Spirit directs us and does not leave us.

His Spirit left with us is the only part of glory we have here on earth to help us look forward to all the riches He has for us in heaven.

REGRETS

I can truly say when I look back on this short life I have no regrets because I did live my life fully for the Lord. I was the best wife I knew how to be and encouraged and worked with my husband. We covered each other's weaknesses, and I tried to make his life and mine the best.

I wanted my children to have the best childhood possible, and I think they have good memories and God was a big part of their lives. We were very close. I believe it is so important for children to have parents who thinks they are great. I led and guided them as a parent, but I also played with them. I was their sounding board when troubles came and a friend to rely on, but I was always their mom. We loved and laughed together; our hearts were one. I don't regret the way I raised my boys because they are good men, and they are great dads. They are raising their kids with a firm hand and lots of love and laughter with God in the center.

The most important thing in my life is God, and I am so happy I am His child. I want to please Him at all times and live my life for Him. I failed at times, but God is merciful. I wanted everyone to know His great love, so I told others about this wonderful God and my Savior Jesus.

Recently, the pastor at my church asked us this question, "If you could do something and would not fail, what would that be?" I thought and thought and everything I ever wanted to do I have done, except one thing, publish this book. I want to publish it because it tells others how they too can live life fully for the Lord. If you are reading this book right now, God has provided for me once more.

When I think back at the things I would change in my life, I wouldn't change a thing. I believe God arranged everything just right. Even my illness I would not change because I believe with out it, I would have lived my life and never known my God personally. I would have been too busy for Him.

I believe my life was like a wood screw that was set the old fashion way with a screwdriver turned by hand. There was the grip, then the turn, and then the release to get another grip, then repeated with another grip, another turn, and another release and so on. The grip was my life held in God's hand, and the turn was Him watching it pass by. The release was the times I was ill and resting in the Lord. I had time to see God in my life during the rest and illness. I was never alone during those times, God was always with me. I am thankful for my life just as it was, and I did live life fully for the Lord.

I had the best relationship with my parents, especially my mom. Most women only wish they had that kind of friendship with their mothers. We were best friends for a lifetime. I chose not to fight or disobey as a child and honored them as the Bible said with no regrets. Their last days were days I was there for them, and I made them an important part of my life. Their memory lives on in me.

Everything I did in my life, I did the best I could. Oh, maybe others could do better than me, but I did it the best I could. I always gave my all to every project I did because I was living for God and gave Him all the glory for the excellence.

I was the best friend I knew how to be. Some say there are two ends to the phone lines; I never thought that, I called my friends even if my friends never called back. I had them over, even if I never went to their homes. I helped them, even when I needed the help myself. I wrote the notes and made the contacts. I did this because I love God and that is what He would want me to do as a friend.

I gave up my time to go to jail, I had people in my home for Bible study, I would listen to friends for hours talk about their troubles and help them to know Jesus. I didn't do it because I thought they needed someone like me, I did it because I love God and that is what He wants us all to do for His people. My love for the Lord is strong and true. I am rooted and grounded in His Word, and I truly believed everything the Bible says.

I remember one Sunday in church, Mrs. Kelpe, an elderly Christian woman who was living in a nursing home, sat in front of me. She had shrunk and was crippled from arthritis and could barely see over the pew now because of old age. I said, "How are you doing today, Mrs. Kelpe?" Her reply was one I will never forget because it is the way I want to be when I am in my eighties or even now. She said, "Oh, I have so much to be thankful for."

Shouldn't we all have the attitude of thankfulness for what we have and not dwell on what we do not? I try to always have a positive attitude and think of my glass as being half full. I cry very little and laugh a lot. There is always someone who is in need and I pray for him or her. I try to remember my life is good no matter how I physically feel.

A full life is one that gives others your time, talent, and treasures. My time is only worth something when it is shared and not hoarded; we need to always know who gives us our time.

I read a book years ago about the gifts God gives us, and at the end of the book there was a test to see what our gifts were. When I took the test, the results were four gifts, and when I realized what gifts I had, I used them. The test showed I was gifted in organization, so I gave retreats for women and was superintendent of the Sunday school. I chair a Christian Women's Club and organize all the luncheons. It comes easy to me because I have the gift. I was gifted in teaching, so I taught Sunday school and Bible studies throughout my life.

Evangelism was the third gift I had, so I told others about Jesus and went to jail. My first pastor recognized this gift in me when I was twenty-five years old. I was excited to tell others about Jesus and was never afraid. To this day when we meet, he asks me if I am still evangelizing the world.

The forth gift was the gift of exhortation. When I was forty-five years old, a mature Christian woman told me I had this gift. I did not quite understand why she said that at the time, until I read the book on gifts a few years later then understood what this gift was. It is the gift of bringing people hope. I do have this gift and used it in jail and at people's bedside and where every there was a need. People need the hope of heaven in their lives knowing we are not alone when we have the Father, Son, and Spirit with us. If we have a gift, we should use it.

I have one more gift that comes from God and that is the gift of writing. He has made me a writer and now an author. I see His presence in this book for it was easy to write. I never knew why I had those hundred or so writings or what I would do with them. And when I started this book, I thought it was for my family and friends. But my God had a bigger plan for all the words I put on paper.

There are some things we need to pray over all the time and those are our family, our pastor, and our church. I believe everyone should be a part of a church so we can be in a family to worship together. When people ask me what religion I am, I say, "I am a Christian and choose to worship in a Lutheran Church." We are all in the body of Christ when we believe in Him. It is easy to be a Christian, all we must do to be in the kingdom of God is believe that Jesus died for our sins and rose again from the dead and lives in heaven with God. Then, call upon the name of the Lord and you will be saved, as the Bible says.

I remember I was at a Lutheran Women's Missionary League meeting, and I was sitting in the back of the room. The speaker asked if anyone was perfect in this room. One woman in the fifth row boldly raised her hand. I was very puzzled because we are all poor miserable sinners. How could she raise her hand like that? At the lunch break, I looked for that women and went to her and asked why she raised her hand. She said, "We are all made perfect by the blood of Jesus when He died for us on the cross." I agreed. My attitude has been different since that day; I live like a forgiven, perfect child of God. Oh, I sin, but I am perfect in God's sight, and that is awesome.

I regret nothing in my life because when I was called, I went. I told others about Jesus in Sunday school, Bible studies, speaking out of town, at retreats, many places, even in jail. These were the best times in my life when I was speaking about Jesus to others. I mentored and counseled and taught others to know the Lord and Savior Jesus Christ. I know many people came to know a Savior because I obeyed God, so I have no regrets.

I prayed for my children, my husband, and my friends. I prayed for God to use me, and He did. I prayed for God to equip me, and I was. Then I prayed the most courageous prayer of all, for God to look deep into my heart and see if He is really there. Did I truly believe what I said about Him to others? My life was bathed in prayer and that is how I spoke to God and He heard my every prayer.

I have learned a lot in my short life, but I know there is still a lot to learn. There is a lesson every day from God if we look to see where He is working in our lives. I want to sing praises to Him and worship Him every day, not just on Sundays. I want to bring Him honor and glory with the things I do and to continue living my life fully for Him. I want Him to never be disappointed in me. At the end of my life, when all is said and done, I want God to say as I enter heaven, "Job well done, good and faithful servant, Patty."